A LEGACY OF TEARS

30 YEARS OF PROTESTANT SUFFERING AT THE
HANDS OF REPUBLICAN TERRORISTS IN
SOUTH AND NORTH ARMAGH 1969-1999

DAVID PATTERSON

Acknowledgements

Project part financed by the Community Relations Council and the European Union through the Special EU Programmes Body

ISBN 1-905281-06-4

Cover design Cedric Wilson
Cover photographs, funerals of Joe Reid, Allen Baird and Roger Love

CONTENTS

This book has been commissioned by the Victim's Group Saver Naver, Bingham House, Main Street, Markethill, Co Armagh.

'In memory of all those innocent victims who lost their lives at the hands of republican terrorists in South and North Armagh.'

Proceeds from the sale of the book will go towards the cost of erecting a Memorial Wall and Garden (at Bingham House) to the innocent victims of republican violence murdered in the South and North Armagh area.

"Where victims are remembered violence cannot be glamourised."

Forward

The conflict in Northern Ireland between 1969-99 resulted in the death of 3,636 people of which 3,376 occurred in Northern Ireland. Statistics provided in the book 'Lost Lives', show that Irish 'republicans' were responsible for 2,139 of the deaths or approximately 60% of the total. The statistics demonstrate that since 1969 terrorism in Northern Ireland was significantly driven by the 'Irish republican' movement.

This republican terrorist onslaught waged against the security forces and civilian citizens of Northern Ireland over the past 30 years has affected, shattered and devastated the lives of thousands of ordinary decent law abiding people.

The reality in Northern Ireland is that the rule of law was sustained over three decades of republican and loyalist terrorism at enormous cost in terms of death and injury on the part of the Royal Ulster Constabulary (RUC) and Ulster Defence Regiment (UDR) in particular, who were operating at the forefront of counter terrorism.

Nowhere was that devastation more pronounced than in South Armagh. During the past 30 years of the Troubles, republicans carried out in South Armagh, 378 murders, were involved in over 1000 bombings and over 1000 gun attacks, resulting in untold carnage, bloodshed and devastation to so many lives. This fanaticism and savagery of Irish republicanism is rooted in what can only be described as a 'cult of violence'.

To add to the pain and loss that so many families suffered at the hands of these evil men is the fact that in the vast majority of these atrocities no one has ever been brought to justice. Adding insult to injury is the Government's determination to grant an amnesty to these terrorists. The tears and the pain behind these stories cry out for justice and for the need to have the perpetrators of these heinous crimes brought before the courts.

It was evident that the lack of justice is deeply distressing to the families affected by the evil deeds of these wicked men and is a stumbling block in allowing them to be able to move on. Yet there is also a deep consciousness within their hearts that ultimately justice will be done when these evil men who may have escaped justice in this world will have to face their Maker.

The stories told and recorded in this book are those of a few of the families in parts of County Armagh associated with the Victims Group SAVER/NAVER who suffered at the hands of the IRA campaign of terror. Their stories are unique and personal to them, but they are also typical of hundreds of similar stories that could be told by so many who also suffered at the hands of republican terrorists.

In the frenzied and immoral pursuit by Government to 'make peace' with the perpetrators of these horrific crimes, the sacrifice of the brave men and women of Ulster, many who made the ultimate sacrifice, has been erased and the true victims of the murderous campaign by republicans have been abandoned and forgotten.

These stories are told in memory of the loved ones lost and as a living and perpetual record of the true story of what was inflicted upon the decent Protestant people of Northern Ireland by the evil and wicked men responsible for over thirty years of republican terrorism.

I have been privileged to be associated with this project. It is, I believe, a vital and important work helping to ensure that the memories of loved ones and the sacrifice that they made is not forgotten, and that the pain, suffering and devastation caused by republican terrorists on the ordinary people of Northern Ireland is recorded for the generations to come.

I appreciate that words can never truly convey the true depth of the suffering experienced. Listening to these stories was a very moving experience that conveyed something of the sense of pain and suffering that was acutely felt in each of the homes that I visited.

While I can never fully empathise with what they have suffered, I do feel an affinity and an empathy with these people since my father served with the RUC in South Armagh throughout the height of the Troubles and witnessed many of these incidents and knew some of the victims.

To see families still so distraught, in many cases after some thirty years, was an experience that I will never forget. I hope that in some small way as I shared with them in their tears as they relived their pain and told their story that somehow the telling of their stories will help them face the future with further steadfastness and courage.

I wish to record my thanks to each of the families who took part for allowing me into their lives at this very emotional and personal level. I will never forget these people and will continue to remember them in their grief and I commend them to the grace of God.

Since this project began some of those who told their stories for this book have passed away and I remember them with fondness.

Pastor David Patterson

The Cup of Hope

We have a little cup that is always on hand
It comforts those who grieve and helps us make a stand
Against all that is evil, for evil thoughts are lost
We look at this cup of hope; we sit and count the cost
Sending our thoughts to God, wondering how He ever coped,
We always get an answer, He always gives us hope
God always sends us assurance in every breath we breathe
As we cling together like birds of a feather
Every class and creed
God will enrich our lives and brings us to His fold
Helping us to bring the victims in from the cold
He will walk down that road with us
And strengthen our willpower
While thinking of the cup of Hope each and every hour
Holding on to that cup of Hope tears will sometimes flow
But yesterday has gone, tomorrow is near
As on with our lives we shall go
Let that crystal cup draw us near, developing friendships along
the way
A cup overflowing with love and kindness, every step of the
way.

Reatha Hassan

The Hale Family

The Hale family, Mr and Mrs Hale and their five children, three girls and two boys, lived and farmed on lands situated on the Dundalk Road, Crossmaglen where the family had been since before the 1860s. Joe Hale, the eldest son, at the age of twenty began an agricultural contracting business in 1960. He purchased the necessary farm machinery and was actively employed doing agricultural contracting work for the whole farming community in South Armagh and in the South of Ireland employed mainly by Roman Catholics. The business thrived and Joe did well and was always kept busy with the contracting work as well as running a dairy herd on the family farm of some sixty-two acres.

Then on 16 August 1969, Joe having worked all day on various farms in the area went in the evening to stock car racing at Portadown. On his return he found the farm sheds ablaze and several fire fighting crews at the premises who despite their best efforts, were unable to put out the fire due to the intensity of the blaze fed by over six thousand bales of hay and around a thousand bales of straw. A combine harvester, two tractors and several other pieces of farm machinery in the shed were also destroyed in the blaze. The fire burned for over a week, nothing could be saved.

Joe's sisters had first come on the fire when they returned from business in Newtownhamiltown and had gone to the local RUC station to report it.

After the farm buildings were burned the family had nothing to live on, there were no benefits and no counselling. The family received no compensation until 1972, and it amounted to only £4 200. The machinery and fodder lost was valued at over £15 000.

Despite this severe disruption to the farm and contracting business, with substantial financial loss and emotional trauma, Joe tried as best he could to pick up the pieces from the burning embers of his business and endeavoured to rebuild the sheds and continue his agricultural contracting business and farming activities.

A year or two before the fire, a farmer from the South for whom Joe had done a lot of contracting work, came to the farm and told the family that he had overheard a conversation in a bar in Dundalk that the Official IRA were trying to acquire a gun to come and shoot Joe Hale because he was supposed to be a member of the 'B' Specials. The farmer said that he would filter back to those sources that their information about Joe Hale was not true; and Joe believes that as a result of that man's intervention the threat must have been lifted.

However in the months following the fire, the family home was bombarded with hate mail, hundreds of letters arriving at the home with implicit and explicit threats about what they were going to do to him. From the day of the fire, neighbours who had always been civil and courteous and who had indeed supported and employed Joe Hale began to ignore the Hale family. People would turn their heads when they met him. Joe reckons that this was most likely because they were told not to speak to him. Rumours were put about that Joe Hale was a member of the 'B' Specials, which was simply not true. None of the Hale family was ever in the security forces nor involved in anything remotely political.

On the Sunday morning after the fire the doctor came out to see Joe who was in a bad way and gave him an injection that put him to sleep for twenty four hours. A Catholic priest not known to the family also visited the family to relay his sympathies.

Both the doctor and the priest told the family that the reason given in the community for the fire was that Joe was supposed to be in the 'B' Specials, but Joe told them that they both would have known for a fact that he was not, nor ever had been, a member of the 'B' Specials.

As a result of this ongoing hate campaign and boycotting of the agricultural contracting business, the Hale's were forced to place their farm on the market. The sale was boycotted. Nobody bid or made any offer for the property for over two years.

The Hale family was continually harassed, cars with full lights driving up to the farm in the middle of the night; people watching the farm and their movements through the day and letting the family know that they were being watched.

During the period that the farm was on the market Joe also

witnessed on his farm the horrific murders of two policemen stationed at Crossmaglen, who were the first two policemen killed by the IRA in the 'Troubles'.

Joe recalled this incident:

> On Sunday morning 10 August 1970, when leaving out the creamery cans at the end of the lane, I noticed a red Mark II Ford Cortina car, fairly new, parked along the side of our land. The next day I had tried unsuccessfully to open the car. I was later drawing hay home from land that I had taken nearby, when I heard a large explosion – the Ford Cortina parked at our land had been booby trapped and exploded killing the two young policemen, Sam Donaldson and Roy Millar who had come to investigate the stolen and abandoned car. I ran into the field where the bodies of these two policemen had been blown by the force of the explosion. One of the policemen spoke, but there was nothing I or anyone could do for them. They were both dying.

The Hale family were affected by this tragedy not just in terms of the emotional trauma. The explosion also impacted upon Joe's farming business. He had sixteen springing heifers, three or four months in calf, grazing in that field and all those heifers lost their calves as a result of the explosion: 'But in comparison to the murder of these two lovely young police lads the loss of livestock was of course insignificant' said Joe.

Eventually in 1972 the state agent purchased the property at £16 200, a price significantly under it's market value. The property was resold two years later to a local farming family with well-known republican links, for over £74 000, plus a further six thousand for a building site. Joe does not believe that this family were in any way responsible for the fire.

The family moved to Markethill and bought a small farm holding of around twenty acres of poor quality land with no out buildings and the dwelling house in need of being rebuilt. This property cost almost the price that they had received for their sixty-two acres with substantial outbuildings and a fine dwelling house in Crossmaglen. The family built a new house, erected outbuildings and brought the land back into high quality. The farm was insufficient to provide a viable income to maintain the family and Joe Hale had to take employment in the Goodyear factory in Craigavon where he worked until the factory closed in 1984.

Joe was unemployed for about a year before finding further employment for about ten years until he broke his back.

This story is one typical of the plight of many Protestant farmers in the border counties during the thirty years of conflict. Growing up in Crossmaglen, Joe said that there were within a two-mile radius approximately forty Protestant families, today there are just two, one a ninety-two year old women. While no life was lost in this incident, the cost in emotional and financial terms is incalculable.

Farming is a way of life, the Hales were robbed of that way of life, and they were robbed of their property that had been in the family from at least 1860. Today Joe's son, who was not born until 1977, several years after these events, still feels robbed of his rightful inheritance which today would be worth in excess of half a million pounds.

Like most of the terrorist crimes in South Armagh no one was ever arrested or brought to account for the burning of the Hale farm, nor the campaign of intimidation mounted against them to drive them out of their homestead. Joe said with a tone of reluctant acceptance, 'I suppose nobody ever will.'

A LEGACY OF TEARS

The impact of the move from the family homestead to Markethill was simply devastating for the family. Joe is convinced that the move almost certainly contributed to his father's death. Joe believes that his father's death in 1977 at the age of sixty-two was as a result of a broken heart caused by the trauma of been driven out of their family home. Joe's brother Frank lost out on his education. Joe suffered depression and had suicidal thoughts for some three years. The depression lasted for a period of ten to twelve years and government and church did nothing to help. Joe said:

> I don't know what the church could have done. Nobody knew what could be done, today we are living in a different age we know a lot more, and more would probably be done today.

> The group has been a tremendous help, it lifted my mind and I have been able to help other people who had been affected to a much greater extent by the 'Troubles' most of them having lost loved ones.

Joe continues, to some extent, to feel greatly grieved and bitter by what happened to him and his family but does not have any thoughts of revenge. Joe concluded:

> I don't think much about them today, my life has moved on, I feel a lot happier now. I am coming to my final period of days here in this world whatever they may be. It's on their conscience to clear themselves or whatever they want to do. Yes I would be willing to forgive them if they were truly sorry and genuinely sought forgiveness.

> At the end of the day the Lord will have to forgive them or they will have to seek their forgiveness from the Lord, my forgiveness will not be any good to them.

Sidney Watt

Sidney Watt lived with his wife Florence and their four children, two girls and two boys, in their home on their farm just outside Newtownhamilton in South Armagh. Sidney was a builder and also ran their small family farm. Sidney served on the 'B' Specials before joining the UDR as a part time soldier.

His son Nigel recalled some of his childhood memories. He spoke of when his father would lift him up and hang him up by his jumper on the rung at the end of their pulley clothesline in their kitchen. He also remembers his father bringing him to Markethill and buying him a pair of hobnail boots and as he walked up and down the shop his daddy saying that they fitted well and he was, 'a great wee man' in them. His father let him carry the boots home in a bag and then when home he put them on and slipped and fell on the cement floor cutting his head. His daddy took him to the doctor who stitched his head and when they came home that was the end of the hobnail boots.

He was never to get another pair of boots from his father.

Another memory was of all the children going to the fields with dad on the trailer behind the tractor and how daddy had tipped the trailer to make a slide for the kids. As the youngest child he was unable to climb up the tipped trailer and so his daddy would lift him up and let him slide down: 'What fun we had.'

Nigel as the youngest child was not yet at school and he remembers being with mum and dad as they fed and saw to the cattle each morning and records how thankful he is for the precious memories that he has, though they were to be so short lived.

Sidney Watt was shot, allegedly by the IRA, on 20 July 1973 at 00.45 am. He was the second UDR man of the Armagh Battalion to be murdered in Northern Ireland. His car was struck by fourteen bullets by gunmen who had lain in wait for him in a gateway opposite his home. Mr Watt was aged just thirty-six when he was murdered. His wife Florence was left a widow at the age of twenty-eight with four small children all under the age of ten.

Mrs Watt recalled that fateful morning:

> On the night of the shooting our four children were in bed sleeping while I was waiting up for my husband to come home from visiting some of our friends. I heard a noise coming from outside and I went to the door. The noise sounded like keys rattling on a window. But to my horror I realised it was shooting and I saw my husband lying at the side of his car. The men who had killed him had searched his car and his

pockets while he lay dying, to see if he had his UDR gun on him. I could see a car parked down the road with its headlights full on, and the gunman kept firing while I was at the door. I ran over to my husband and the gunman ran off down the road to the waiting car.

Sidney was still alive at this time. He spoke a few words and I ran into the house to get a cushion and put it under his head. He said his leg hurt and that he was cold. Sidney warned me not to go near the crossroads as he lay dying. Our car and the walls of our house were riddled with bullets and one bullet had cut the electric wire leaving us without electricity.

I was in such a shocked and dazed dilemma that I did not know what to do so I just gently put my arms around my dear husband and held him, trying to comfort him. This was the way I was left for a very long time until a car came along and I stopped it and asked the people in the car, a father and daughter, if they could get me help as my husband had been shot. At this time I had no telephone and where I lived was isolated. The man who came to my aid drove into Newtownhamilton Police barracks to report the shooting and get us help, and his daughter stayed with me.

It seemed a very long time before the ambulance came and then the army arrived. They took Sidney away in the ambulance and it was my belief my husband was dead at this stage, although I did not know for sure. I was numb and void of any feelings. It was like the worst nightmare you could imagine. The police never came out to me, but the army and an ambulance arrived at the same time. Here there is a blankness with me. I cannot remember who it was that lifted Sidney into the ambulance, or the ambulance driving away. The army stayed around the house for the rest of the night.

The young women who stopped to help me, stayed with me,

and the two of us were in a state of shock. We went into my house and made a cup of tea and went to bed. I did not know what to do. My world was turned upside down. Then at about 3.30 am, my parents and brother and sister arrived to tell me that my husband was dead on arrival at hospital. There are so many things I cannot remember about all that happened on that night.

I can remember my two daughters waking up in a very distressed state and me trying to comfort and settle them back into bed. The children knew there was something awful wrong. They sensed the turmoil and pain. I still could not take all this in; it was real, it was such a nightmare.

My minister, Rev Murphy, and his wife arrived, and it was Mrs Murphy who broke the news to my children: four, six, seven and ten years old. This was heart breaking.

Nigel the youngest boy only four at the time recalled this awful moment:

Mrs Murphy came to our house one morning and my brother, sisters and myself were sitting on the bed. She told us our father was dead and had gone to heaven. I remember her saying that bad men had shot him and that he had died on the way to hospital. Daddy was not brought home at that time. I don't think I understood until I saw the coffin in my bedroom. I could not go in to look at my father. I can remember I did not want to go into that room for a long time.

I also remember a lot of people at the house and my fathers coffin and lots and lots of people behind it. When I was older I understood that what I had seen was the funeral of my father.

A LEGACY OF TEARS

The funeral service, attended by hundreds of mourners, was to the local family church at Ballymoyer. At the funeral service the local minister said that it was neither a time for words of recrimination nor the place for a political speech. He said the crime had, 'trodden down our civilised way of life' and 'crushed underfoot democracy, respect for fellow man, human decency and consideration for others.'

The generous and caring nature of Mrs Watt was seen in her request that money in lieu of flowers was to be given in aid of UDR Welfare.

The lives of this little family were devastated. Life would never be the same again. Mrs Watt relayed some of the difficulties of those days following the murder of her husband:

> I was now left with four young children to rear on a small farm with no help and no money. I was not in the best of health, as I had just suffered a miscarriage and I found it very difficult to cope and manage. My husband was killed in July and I did not get the pension until the end of that year, and then it was only the Second World War rate. It was a further two years before I received compensation of £8 250, and nothing at all for my four children.
>
> At the time of Sidney's death our home was not fully completed. The building work was complete but other work had still to be carried out, and there was money owing on it and bills to be paid. I was determined to keep and make a home for my children, so out of the compensation money I paid what was owed on the house, and put £2 000 away for my children. The stress and strain of managing everything, and the post trauma stress of Sidney's murder, took its toll on my health.

Despite having robbed this family of a husband and father, the evil minds of republican terrorists continued to afflict this family in an attempt to now drive them from their home:

> Twelve years after Sidney was killed, a bomb was left at our home. The INLA admitted leaving this bomb. They claimed that my two sons, one seventeen and the other nineteen were members of the UDR. This was not true. My sons were never in the UDR. This was a blatant attack of intimidation to move us out of our home and it succeeded in breaking us.

> The police had informed Nigel, my youngest son that a bomb was going to be left at the house. This was one week before the bomb was planted and we put in a dreadful time of anxiety. We were afraid to cross the yard in the farm, in case there were wires leading to an explosive device and we had to check the cars going out and coming in. During this week my sons and I never received any police protection. Exactly one week later I found the bomb in a lunch box behind my car, which was sitting at the side of our house. I informed the police at 8.30 in the morning and it wasn't until at least 3.30 in the afternoon that they and the army arrived to check this out.

The bomb was later defused and the police told the family that if it had gone off, whoever was in the car would have been killed and most likely the house would have been damaged if not destroyed possibly causing further death and injury to those who were there:

> My whole nervous system was shattered and I was living in such fear for each of our lives. By this stage my two daughters had married and moved away, one living in Scotland. I borrowed money from a neighbour and my sons and I went to Scotland in the hope of starting a new life there. A friend

promised to look after my home and the cattle. However we stayed in Scotland only a few weeks and had to return home as all the farms we viewed capable of providing a reasonable income for the family, were far beyond our means.

When the family returned from Scotland they were back to square one and with no money. Mrs Watt had to get a job and start all over again in an attempt to make a life for herself and her two sons.

Even after Nigel married and went to live in Tynan, quite some distance from Newtownhamilton, he continued to receive threatening phone calls and on a number of occasions was followed home especially when visiting his mother at their home and helping her about the house and farm.

The suffering that this family endured at the hands of terrorists is, except for those like them who have come through similar experiences, beyond comprehension. They were left by and large to cope alone:

> Counselling was unknown at the time and the only relief I found was through medication prescribed by my doctor. Thankfully in time I was able to wean myself off the medication and was enabled to throw myself into working and maintaining my children and our little farm and home.

> Thankfully now there is some help and counselling available for people like my family and me.

I conclude this story with words from Nigel:

> I have to say that at four and a half years old no one ever thinks how a child copes with the sudden disappearance

through murder, of his dearly loved father. I never received any help in anyway. This led to many thoughts going through my head and no answers to any of them. This is how I walked on in life, holding on to my pain and distress.

Since recording this story Mrs Watt who had been suffering from cancer has passed away.

Joseph Reid

Joseph Reid was born on 19 January 1927 at the family home at Fernaloy just outside Keady, county Armagh.

As a young man Joe played the violin in a family dance band known as the 'Buffs' which consisted of his father William on the drums, brother George, accordion and half brother Jimmy also playing violin. Joe was a successful farmer and a respected and widely known agricultural contractor. His work took him near and far, summer and winter, and both sides of the community employed him and for those who employed him his word was his bond.

On 6 April 1953 Joe was married to Irene Foster of Kilcreevy, in First Keady The Temple Presbyterian Church by Rev John Mark. They lived in the family home with Joe's parents and had five children, one son, Noel and four daughters Iris, Pamela, Gladys and Jennifer.

As a family man Joe was faithful in attending church with his wife and children. His love of music continued through his life and he and his wife attended many functions and dances in local country halls. Often on a Sunday evening Joe would take the family for a drive to the coast and they would enjoy picnics in some of the forest parks.

Joe was a member of the Kirk of Session of the Temple Church, a unionist member of Armagh District Council and a prominent Orangeman. Joe was loyal and faithful to his local Orange Lodge, Crosskeys LOL 88 in which he had been a Past Worshipful Master and helped organise and run many of the fund raising events. He was also a member of the Armagh County Grand Lodge; treasurer of Keady District LOL No 8; Worshipful Master of Tassagh Royal Black Preceptory; a member of Crosskeys Flute Band; and a member of Zetland Masonic Lodge, Keady.

In 1970 when his family were still young and the Troubles were increasing, he became a part time soldier of 'A' Company of the 2nd battalion of the UDR to fight for his Queen and country. He gained the rank of lance corporal.

Mrs Reid spoke of the dedication involved:

> After a hard days work he would go on duty as a part time soldier serving his country in the best way he thought possible. For Joe like so many of his comrades, joining the UDR was not for financial gain, as with so many other commitments he did not need the extra task of duty two and three nights a week, but that was what he felt he should do. The family knew that they lived in troubled times, hay sheds were being burned

and they felt vulnerable as a Protestant farming family living
near the predominantly nationalist border area of Keady.

Although the family did not feel that Joe's life was under any
specific threat they like other security force families had to take
precautions such as looking under the car for suspicious objects.
The children recalled going down to the gate to wave their daddy
out at the junction while pretending to play. At the time they were
told to go and check if there was any traffic coming, not really
knowing why, but looking back they now realise that it was to make
sure their father could drive straight out from the farm gate and on
to the road.

On 'Black Saturday' 30 August 1975, Joe walked proudly in front
of Tassagh Royal Black Preceptory in Armagh and Aughnacloy.
The following day, Sunday, his duty as a part time soldier took
him to South Armagh where one of his comrades had been brutally
murdered. An hour after arriving home and preparing for bed, one
of his daughters answered a knock at the front door at which were
two men. The man leaning against the porch wall, wearing a black
knitted cap asked, 'Is Joe in?' Joe's daughter called upstairs for her
father and went into the kitchen. A few seconds later, gunfire was
heard and Joe staggered into the kitchen and fell to the floor. Joe
never spoke, his pistol fell from his hand, the glass in the front
door was shattered and bullets pierced the wall of the sitting room
where his son had been watching television. His daughters tried
in vain to stem the flow of blood from his chest, as Joe's elderly
father shook his head and said, 'It's no good.'

Joe had been fatally wounded nine times, mainly to his chest. His
son ran with his mother to telephone for the doctor and in their
panic and not being able to get a connection, they believed the
phone lines had been cut. His son ran out of the house and went to

his aunt's house nearby to tell the terrible news and phone for the doctor.

The scene in the home was horrific; blood everywhere and everyone in total shock. Soon the house filled with people, the doctor, ambulance men, police, UDR, relatives and neighbours.

The two younger children who had been upstairs heard the gunfire but were too afraid to venture down not knowing what had happened and thinking the gunmen may still be there. They remained in their bedroom until a relative came to take them away. The three younger children stayed with relatives over the next few days and were shielded from newspaper reports and TV coverage and did not attend the funeral. At the time this was considered to be the best for them by well meaning and caring relatives.

Next day in news bulletins the South Armagh 'Brigade' of the Provisional IRA claimed responsibility for Joe's murder.

Hundreds of people, including relatives and neighbours as well as many people the family did not know, visited the family home to pay their respects to a man they held in high esteem. Among these were dignitaries of the Church, political parties, council representatives and heads of security forces offering comfort to the family and expressing disgust at the murder. A hundred and thirty-two wreaths covered the family garden. The funeral service held in the family church at the Temple conducted by the Rev John Mark was attended by thousands of people. The funeral cortege stretched endlessly as it winded its way through the countryside to the church. At the service Rev Mark paid tribute to Joe and likened him to David in the Bible and his message was, 'the steps of a good man are ordered by the Lord.' (Psalm 37:23) Joe was aged forty-eight.

Joe's father, William, lived for another six years and was looked after by Irene until his death in 1981. This was a trying and difficult time for Irene.

The family lived in fear, but, as always on a farm, work had to be done and everyone had to help out. Life was never to be the same again. As the winter and darker nights approached, fear and terror remained with the family and as relatives and friends returned to their own families and work, the Reid family became just another part of the ugly jigsaw of violence, hatred, bitterness and fear.

The family were bitter they had hatred and hardness in their hearts, because evil men, whom they will never forgive, had taken away someone they loved.

Yet within the home the incident was never openly talked about, nor feelings expressed. Life had to go on, and the children returned to school and work. Over thirty years on and still no one has been charged with Joe's murder. The family have so many unanswered questions:

> Where is the gunman and his accomplice, what are they doing now, have they families of their own, are they proud of what they did? Someone out there knows, someone knows.

No one will ever be able to measure the extent to which the family and community were impoverished by the cruel murder of Joe Reid. Joe was not permitted to live to see his five children grow up and marry. His children were deprived of a father who would have been so proud of them on their wedding days. As a result wedding days were always sad and difficult occasions for Irene and her family, as well as for the family of the respective bride and grooms.

A LEGACY OF TEARS

Joe was never to see his children build new lives for themselves nor to experience the joy of sharing with his twenty grandchildren and one great grandchild.

The family live with the pain, the heartache, but hold dear memories of a husband and a father they are proud of and miss always. They concluded with these words:

'Silent tears still fall.'

Funeral of Joseph Reid

Bobby Freeburn

Mr Bobby Freeburn lived near Bessbrook with his wife Anna and children Alan and Sandra. The life of this family was cruelly shattered by one of the most brutal and sectarian acts of barbarianism perpetrated by the IRA. This indescribable atrocity was the massacre of ten Protestant workmen who were callously lined up and shot by the IRA. Approximately twelve IRA gunmen lay in wait at Kingsmills near Bessbrook in South Armagh on a January evening in 1976 as the workmen were returning home from work in a minibus. This barbaric act was carried out against these ten men simply because they were Protestants.

Mrs Freeburn who now lives in Canada takes up the story of that night:

Monday 5 January 1976 will be a day that will be forever etched on the minds of our family. It was a normal working day in the lives of the employees of John Compton's factory at Glenanne. The usual routine for our family was for my son, Alan to meet the Glenanne factory minibus in Bessbrook and bring my husband Bobby home to our house, approximately two miles from Bessbrook. That night the bus was late, so my son decided he would drive to meet the bus, only to be stopped by a police check point on the Kingsmills Road. Little did he know that about a half a mile further along the road there lay ten bodies murdered by terrorists. Their bus was stopped by a red light, which was quite normal, as the security forces used red lights to stop traffic; this was not a security check point. The men were asked to line up against the bus and asked their names and one worker, a Catholic, was asked to step forward and keep walking. One man, Alan Black survived and lives everyday with the memories of that night.

Life in our family changed from that night on. The breadwinner of the family gone, children left without a father and myself learning to cope with life as a widow. No help, counselling, financial or otherwise was offered from the Government. We had to face and cope as best we could with this situation we found ourselves in. Our faith played and still does play a big part in our survival.

Eleven years ago my son, daughter-in-law and two grandsons left Northern Ireland to make a new life for themselves in Canada. Three years ago my daughter and I followed them. My children have been robbed of their father, my grandsons did not get the opportunity to get to know their grandfather, they have left the land of their birth because the future in Northern Ireland did not offer them safety, security and a life of peace. Only when Northern Ireland and its people return to their Creator and realise that true and lasting peace can only come when God is given first place in their lives will the situation be truly resolved. Northern Ireland will always have a special place in our hearts and we continue to pray for that land and its people.

This is a brief story of a woman's faith and courage in the wake of an appalling atrocity that robbed her of her husband and her children of a father.

Many years later Anna's suffering was compounded by the need to have her left leg amputated. However with the help of her daughter Sandra she has been able to lead a fairly normal life. Anna and Sandra were greatly helped through the work of the group SAVER/NAVER and indeed received much pleasure from their regular attendance at the meetings, often travelling weekly from Bessbrook to Markethill to attend the meetings and activities of the Group.

In 2002 Anna and Sandra decided to move to Canada to where Alan had emigrated a number of years before. Being together again as a family brought Anna and the whole family much joy and happiness.

However, providence was to deal another blow when Anna's health deteriorated and she had to have her other leg amputated and then had a hip replacement. Yet as before, Anna with the help of God and the support of her family, has been enabled once again to live her life to the best of her ability.

Sandra, had qualified as a dental nurse in Northern Ireland and worked in Northern Ireland for Dr Martin Maltese. However when she went to Canada, Sandra discovered that her qualifications were not recognised in Canada and consequently is having to do all her examinations again. This is costing Sandra over $6 000 and a lot of study.

If the Kingsmills massacre had not happened the Freeburn family would probably still have been living in Bessbrook. But like so many families in South Armagh, the personal impact of republican terrorism upon their lives has devastated, disrupted and displaced this family forever.

Yet through the entire trauma Anna bears a living testimony, like so many others, to the fact that her faith in God has sustained the family through all the dark and difficult days thrust upon them by this dastardly act of evil and wicked men.

John McConville

The McConville family Tommy and Esther, with their four children, John, Karen, Mandy and Tania lived at 30 Moninna Park, Cloughrea, about two miles from the village of Bessbrook. Karen, the eldest daughter spoke of her childhood memories growing up in Bessbrook as, 'by and large happy, treasured times.'

Bessbrook was a close knit rural community and a model industrial village, initiated by Quakers in the eighteenth century. The McConville children enjoyed a happy childhood; playing in the countryside and spending time with their grandmother and her sister.

The family attended the local Presbyterian church, where the children were involved in Sunday school as well as the afternoon Sunday school in the local Gospel Hall. Boys Brigade and Girls

Guides also played an important role in their lives during their formative years; organisations that provide for, and nurture the needs of the whole person; practically, socially, physically and spiritually.

Village life was most harmonious and although two diverse religions lived side by side, the McConville children grew up in an environment in which they were not aware of any tensions or divisions between the two communities.

Mrs McConville and daughter Karen described John as, 'a gentle, caring considerate and fun loving young boy.' They recalled his sense of humour and the constant flow of laughter with his sisters through childhood and teenage years, as they bantered and played pranks on each other continually, much to the dismay of their mother.

John became a Christian at the age of sixteen and sometime following his conversion became a member of Newry Baptist Church. John's only desire was to go to Bible College to prepare for missionary work in South Africa to which he believed God was calling him. He enrolled on and completed various Bible correspondence courses in which he gained distinctions. He also sought to be a faithful and inspiring advocate for Christ. John would faithfully, in the most practical and unassuming way, seek to share God's Word with all whom he met. His faith in God and subsequent witness was a great inspiration to all who knew him. Touching many lives, across the community divide, by his honest and humble ministry.

At the age of twenty John was accepted at a Bible College in Scotland where he was to commence full time study in the autumn of 1976. He was noticeably delighted and shared with the family how he felt so sure that this was God's plan for his life.

To save up for the college fees, John had taken a job at Compton's Spinning Mill at Glenanne about four miles from Bessbrook where he worked for about two years.

On the 5 January 1976, the 'Mill's' minibus set off to return twelve workers to their homes. John Mc Conville was among the passengers on that minibus. As the vehicle wended its way along the dark, lonely country roads of South Armagh, its happy occupants were having a very normal conversation about a recent football match. The conversation also turned to the tragic events of the previous night when two Roman Catholic brothers had been shot and killed at their home in nearby Whitecross.

As the minibus approached the brow of a hill near to Kingsmill crossroads, a red torchlight was spotted by the driver, who slowed down and stopped, believing this to be a routine army check. Men wearing combat jackets, with their faces blackened, immediately joined the man waving the torch.

The occupants were ordered out of the minibus and were asked to state their religion. Initially the one Roman Catholic passenger was thought to be the intended target, but when the gang ordered him to run, it was quickly realised by the Protestant passengers that only his life was to be spared.

The remaining eleven workmen were then lined up at gunpoint along the side of the minibus, and ten of them were slain in a hail of gunfire. One man, though badly wounded, survived the attack and was able later to relate the horrific event that saw his colleagues murdered.

That evening, Mrs McConville had returned from work and had made the tea when she heard on the television news that there had been an incident involving a minibus. Mrs McConville immediately said to her husband Tommy, 'John's on that minibus.' Tommy told her to phone the police and enquire, but when she phoned Bessbrook RUC station they couldn't tell her anything and asked her to ring back later. Mrs McConville then asked her husband to take her out to Kingsmill, though at this time she did not think about death, she simply thought that maybe it was some kind of an accident. Her husband agreed to take her to a neighbours house, Mrs McWhirter, whose husband would also have been on the minibus:

> Mrs McWhirter came to the door and related that she had also heard about the minibus incident. She asked me to make her a wee cup of tea and Tommy went up to the police station. When Tommy returned some time later he had no further information about the incident and I insisted that he take me out to Kingsmill. We went out to the scene where a policeman, Constable Billy Turbitt who was also to be abducted and murdered by the IRA in 1978, stopped us. We told him who we were, and explained to him that our son was on the minibus and could he tell us what had happened. Constable Turbitt told us that he couldn't, but to pull our car in to the side of the road. At that point three ambulances arrived at the scene and Constable Turbitt told us that the best thing to do was to follow the ambulances into Daisy Hill hospital in Newry.

Tommy and Esther followed the ambulances to the hospital where they met one of the ambulance drivers, Stuart Roland and asked him, 'what about John?' He said that he couldn't tell them, but said that their daughter Karen was at the hospital.

Mrs McConville had left the three girls at home and told them not to move, but they had heard further news on the radio about the incident and Karen, the eldest daughter, had gone up to her uncle's and asked him to take her to the hospital. As soon as Mrs McConville entered the hospital, she met their local minister the Rev Nixon. With tears Mrs McConville recalled how he just caught her by the two arms and said, 'John's gone.'

They waited in a room and Rev Nixon gave Mrs McConville a tablet as a doctor and a policewoman arrived to offer help. The family then headed home to find it overflowing with neighbours; many of them Roman Catholics. Tommy went over to College Square to break the news to Esther's mother, and brought her over to the house where, overcome by grief, she took a 'turn.' The intensity of the family's grief was at times uncontrollable. Karen at times screamed such was her grief and anguish.

Mrs McConville was in such shock that she did not know the details of how her son had been killed and thought that it had been a road accident involving the mini bus. She later had to be told of how her son, along with ten other Protestants, were taken from the minibus, lined up and gunned down in cold blooded murder. A policeman who arrived first at the scene described it as an, 'indescribable scene of carnage.' Ten men including John McConville, lay dead on the road. One of the victims, though shot eighteen times, survived.

More than three thousand people attended the funeral services of the ten murder victims. The funeral service for John McConville was held jointly with five other victims of the massacre in Bessbrook Presbyterian Church on the 8 January 1976 amidst driving rain, and his body laid to rest in the adjoining graveyard.

A LEGACY OF TEARS

The day of the funeral was extremely wet, the church was filled to overflowing and Dr Paisley and Rev McCrea vacated their seats for Mrs McConville.

Sitting listening to Mrs McConville tell the story of her grief and perusing through the hundreds of sympathy cards, the newspaper articles, a beautiful inscribed Bible presented in John's memory and the children's hymn written especially for children in Northern Ireland and published by the John McConville Memorial Trust, was a most moving experience. I was aware of a very real sense of grief still abiding in that home and in the hearts of the family.

Derrick Bingham a well known Brethren preacher, later wrote in a Christian magazine this tribute to John: 'He was a quiet lad who had a real and happy faith in the Lord Jesus. Uncomplicated, like Caleb, he wholly followed the Lord.' In the article Derrick Bingham recalled reading in the flyleaf of John's Bible as he stood by John's open coffin these words: 'It is the praising heart in prayer that can expect great things from God'. Mr Bingham wrote: 'It was a praising heart that was murderously silenced – yet in the eternal Kingdom it is a heart that now praises as it never did before.'

Mrs McConville became a Christian at the time of the murder and believes that only by God's grace and her faith in Christ was she able to cope and to keep going.

After the incident Mandy and Tania, the youngest, experienced nervous reactions as a result of their grief and had to attend the hospital. Mrs McConville tells of how another lady in the hospital at that time, suffering from cancer, asked to speak to her and the lady became a Christian as a result.

The following June the McConvilles moved house to Riverside

Crescent in Bessbrook, as they felt it impossible to stay in their home at Moninna Park and that a move might in some small way help.

Karen, the eldest girl, felt it impossible to stay in Bessbrook and moved to work and live in Belfast.

Mrs McConville had to go on antidepressants and returned to work just two weeks after the murder: 'It was a terrible time, it was awful, I wouldn't wish it on anybody. I just had to go on. Only by God's help did I get through it.'

At that time there was no counselling offered or available, but the family found great help and support in their minister, the Rev Nixon, not only at the time of John's murder, but continuing throughout his ministry in the local Presbyterian church: 'He would faithfully and regularly visit the family to offer comfort and reassurance through those dark and difficult times.'

Mrs McConville and her family, like so many others, have found the strength to go on, but still keenly feel a great sense of pain and loss. Yet they bear no bitterness or resentment to the evil perpetrators of this most atrocious crime. Like dozens of murders in county Armagh, no one has been brought to the courts or convicted of the Kingsmill massacre. Mrs McConville is content to leave justice to God before whom all men must one day give an account, but has a longing to know: 'Who did it? 'Who killed my son?'

Daughter Karen records:

> Evil men had in the most brutal and inhuman way extinguished the life of John in his prime and I am going to

miss him for the rest of my life.

The loss of John has taught me many things, not least the sanctity and preciousness of life. I had been forced into a position where I was confronted with the effects of the hatred, revenge and intolerance of certain members of society that had claimed the lives of innocent people. If John and his companions were murdered in order to create further hatred within society then for that reason I would not allow myself to be so influenced.

I have learned to leave justice, retribution and revenge in the hands of the Lord. This is a great comfort to me, as I know that God will have the final say as far as the perpetrators of this evil deed are concerned. More so considering that no one has been charged with the Kingsmill murders.

Although these men walk free, they are tethered to this dreadful event for the remainder of their lives.

I on the other hand can remember my dear brother with pride, happiness and admiration for his devotion, tolerance and love. He is in a much better place and for this I am happy. No one can take him or these memories away from me ever again.

Joe Wilson

Mr Joe Wilson lived on a small nine acre holding at 37 Lisdown Road, Armagh with his wife Anna and nine children, Jim, Florence, Ann, Isobel, Barbara, Harold, Robert, Ruth and John.

Mr Joe Wilson worked at Lester's shop in Armagh and served as a part time soldier in the UDR in which he held the rank of lieutenant. Mr Wilson had previously served on the 'B' Specials until they were disbanded in 1969. He also ran the small family farm.

Joe Wilson was a hard working family man who loved each of his children and worked 'night and day' to provide for them as best he could.

The family fondly remember a dear husband and loving father:

> Every morning he would have been out across the fields at

six o'clock rain, hail or snow bringing in the cows to milk. He followed the cows into the yard with his hand on the back of the 'white' cow. That was after coming in off duty with the UDR at maybe two or three in the morning. Yet in all his years he never failed to have 'Lester's shop where he worked opened at 8.30 am. Joe was a man who loved his family. When I was in Lurgan hospital expecting some of the children and some of the women would ask the nurses if their men were there. The nurses would look out and say, 'I don't know but there's one baldy headed man here any way and he can't wait to get in to see his child.' That was Joe. Joe was frustrated that he could not do all that he wanted to do – money was scarce, and he was working all hours. Working eight to six, coming home getting his tea and out to do the 'turns' on the farm as he called them, and a way out on duty at eight o'clock to three o'clock sometimes four or five nights a week.

On 15 September 1972 the Wilson family home was raided by the IRA. At 9.30 am four masked and armed men broke into the home at Lisdown and held a pistol to Mrs Wilson's head and threw her baby from it's cot to the floor before making off with UDR uniforms and a shotgun.

Mrs Wilson told how she was upstairs in her home on the morning of the raid with her four year old son and eighteen month old granddaughter when she looked out of a window and noticed a turquoise car coming along the road and stopping at her house. The men got out of the car one of whom were carrying a 'big gun' and the other a small one. Then she heard the door smash open and the two men came upstairs. One man put a gun to her cheek and the other man went to the baby's room and threw the one and half year old baby from the cot unto the floor. They then searched the wardrobe and took her husband's uniform and a shotgun.

Though the men were partly masked, Mrs Wilson recognised one of the men as 'McQuade' from the 'Shambles' area of Armagh and later identified him at Portadown RUC station.

From this time on the Wilson family were plagued with threats and had to be under permanent twenty-four hour police and UDR protection and remained so for some two years. Mrs Wilson was not even able to go shopping without police protection and her son John had to be taken to school by a neighbour:

> There were all these IRA threatening letters – one read 'Threat to Wilson family' and warned that my husband Joe was to be shot in the near future. Another letter said that 'there are four ways into your house but they all go in through the one gate.'

Then on 11 September 1975 there was an attempt on the life of her husband by four youths as he went to his car in the Shambles yard. They fired four or five shots at him from close range hitting him in the chest but he was not seriously injured. Mr Wilson was able to go to his work at the supermarket the next day. Two youths were later jailed for this attempted murder.

The family were then advised to move from their home in the country to the town but Mr Wilson refused to move because, 'he loved the country and he loved his children, those times we were living on nothing, but he died without any debt.'

Mrs Wilson, with tears, recalled the day of the 26 October 1976 when her husband Joe, aged fifty-three, was murdered:

> Isobel and her child called and took Joe and me into town. We left Joe off at the shop in the Shambles and he forgot his

lunch box and we shouted after him. But he was not to need it. Isobel and I then called for Barbara and went shopping. We had to get the child, Colin, a new duffle coat and Joe had asked us to get a prize for something the UDR was running. He had said £5 no more, but eventually we got a Tyrone crystal bowl for £6 and the coat.

We were going back round to the shop to show Joe the purchases and when we were going up College Street we saw the police cars flying past us and I said you father's been shot and when we went round the corner we met the ambulance taking Joe to hospital.

We went on up to the shop and saw the scene with the blood lying where they had shot him and where they had carried him out. I went berserk and the doctor, Dr Spence, came. He had Joe's watch and give it to me and gave me an injection and assured me Joe would be all right. But he was already gone. Harold had been contacted and was at the City hospital watching through the door as they pumped the blood into him but all to no avail.

They then took me round to Barbara's where people were beginning to gather. Jim who was on duty in Belfast with the RUC, heard about his father's murder over the police radio. We headed out to Lisdown and met the two family dogs a Springer and a Labrador heading into the town. The dogs never left the house. It seemed by instinct they knew that something had happened to Joe.

Joe's son, Harold, had just delivered bread to the shop where his father worked and had left to return to the bakery in Armagh to reload the bread van, when someone, he doesn't know who, phoned the depot to say that his father had been shot.

When the family came to Armagh Technical school to take Robert out and tell him about his father, pupils in the class shouted, 'I hope it's your f……. fathers been murdered.' Robert had to be taken permanently from the school because of ongoing physical and verbal abuse including acid being thrown at him.

John who was only seven or eight years old ran away and hid when he was told of his father's murder.

Joe Wilson was the thirteenth member of the 2nd Co. Armagh battalion to be killed by republican terrorists, and the 62nd UDR victim over the four-year period since the formation of the UDR in 1972.

Hundreds of mourners attended the funeral service to Knappagh Presbyterian Church, making it one of the largest funerals of a member of the security forces killed since the troubles began. At the funeral service the Moderator of the Presbyterian Church, Dr Jack Weir, said: 'The attack on one in Mr Wilson's position, or anyone who sought to do the duty laid on him or expected of a citizen by the community, was an attack on every one who sought for peace and order, and justice under the law, whatever their church or background, their political hopes or fears.'

The minister of Knappagh Presbyterian Church where Joe worshipped so often, the Rev W S Martin who was deeply saddened by the murder, speaking at the funeral service commented that: 'Joe Wilson did not content himself to live life in an ordinary fashion, but gave his time, indeed his life for our community.' At the graveside Mrs Wilson in deep anguish cried out, 'It should never have happened.'

In what one might describe as an unbelievably callous act, local republican youths attempted to set Joes's car on fire on the night of the funeral service where it was parked at the front of the house.

Over the following weeks and months black bows and bullets were left on the hedgerows of the garden:

> The effect of Joe's death upon the family was enormous. Trying to keep things going, the debts started. The animals had to be sold to meet the bills. Four children were still at home and no breadwinner. The place had to be sold and the family moved into the town due to the continual threats against them. The phone number was changed four times and every time 'republicans' got the number and constantly phoned to harass and threaten the family about what was going to happen to them. But how and ever we are still here. There's a God above and that's it and He has looked after me and the children through all my trials and tribulations, but as I said the day of the funeral it never should have happened. It has been an awful time. When I came in here, it was terrible.

Harold's wedding was arranged for the following February and Mrs Wilson can hardly remember being at it:

> We had the upheaval of moving, bills to pay. Robert was on the UDR and I had to sit to three in the morning waiting for him to come in, desperate. Harold had to leave the bread run and join the UDR full time because it was too dangerous to remain on the bread van.

Mrs Wilson said: 'We had to forget about the circumstances and not allow ourselves to become bitter.' Catholic clergy who visited the home asked if they were bitter and said that she was a wonderful women: 'But we had to move on; we had to get on with our lives. You just wonder why?'

The family's problems did not end with the murder of Joe. Barbara's husband, Herbie Burrows, an undertaker, was targeted and killed by the IRA on 3 March 1984 when a booby trapped bomb left at his place of work exploded. Another son Jim, an RUC detective, was also injured by a Catholic mob in Belfast while on duty.

Mrs Wilson had by and large to cope alone with the consequences of the evil deed of the IRA murderers who robbed her of a wonderful husband, her children of a great father, and the whole community of a good man. Mrs Wilson acknowledged that:

> The UDR was very supportive; the police were also excellent. At the time the family got only £5000 compensation. The UDR is good to me I still go for a week to Portrush and Bangor.

> The church was a great help, the minister at that time was great, they could not have done more.

The family do look back with pride on their loved one who was brutally and callously murdered simply because he was a Protestant who sought to serve his country. In the church at Knappagh there is a plaque in memory of Joe presented by his UDR company in 1977.

However, this memorial and the pride that they feel cannot relieve the family of their intense grief. Thirty years later the family still feel the pain every day; through many tears Mrs Wilson recalled her story. Yet the resolve and courage of this family like so many others is truly remarkable and stands in marked contrast to the evil and cowardice of the perpetrators of this murder. The perpetrators have never been brought to account for their dastardly crime.

Mrs Wilson said, 'But you have to go on. The group is marvellous; you can go up at any time get a cup of tea and a chat. Invaluable.'

In closing this chapter I quote the words of one son Harold: 'Somebody did it and they will have to meet their Maker.'

The Wilson family home at Lisdown Road, Armagh.

Allen Baird

The Baird family from the little sleepy village of Scarva in county Armagh, look back over three generations of service in Northern Ireland's security forces, stretching right back to the establishment of Northern Ireland in 1920. Leslie Baird's father, William, was one of the first recruits to the newly formed RUC in 1922. Leslie himself served for twenty-five years on the 'B' Specials and recalled doing border patrols in South Armagh from 7 pm until 5 am for sixteen shillings a night: 'It was cold, wet and dangerous but I was defending my country.'

Leslie's son Allen, the second boy of a family of seven, (three girls and four boys) joined the RUC in 1976. Three years later at the young age of twenty-eight and married with two young children he was brutally murdered by the IRA.

Allen began what was to be a very brief career in the RUC when he first joined the RUC Reserves part time in 1975 serving in Banbridge station. At that time Allen worked as a bar man in his wife's grandmother's bar in Banbridge know as 'McKees'. Allen was a very bright boy at school, had passed his eleven plus and was interested in getting on in life.

Allen then joined the regular RUC force in 1976 and was designated to Bessbrook station in South Armagh.

Allen was a great family man. He married Alwyn Smith from Banbridge and had come to live at 20 Main Street, Scarva, just a couple of doors from the home of his father and mother. They had two children, Gordon and Judith who were just seven and three years old when their father was cruelly murdered in the prime of life. He was a good father to his two children. Every night without fail he came to visit his mother and would stay for about an hour. He had been as usual in their house the night before he was killed. His father was standing at the door the next morning when Allen left to go to his work and his father waved to him as he drove off in the car. Little did Leslie know that would be the last time he would ever see his son. Leslie recalls the events of that terrible day:

> I remember the day vividly, it was Easter Tuesday, 17 April 1979. I was up the garden putting in some potatoes and had just finished and come down into the house and the Misses said hurry up it's a good day lets go for a bit of a drive.

> Then I went into the other room where there was a radio that had not been going for some time and I said to myself I wonder is that still working. So I switched it on and the one o'clock news came on. My wife and Allen's wife were standing in the

hall. The first thing on the news was that there had been an explosion in Bessbrook and some policemen had been killed.

We knew Allen was on duty and the two women just jumped to the conclusion that it was Allen. I tried to calm them down and said that we don't know who has been killed, hold on a minute and I'll ring the station and find out.

I rang Bessbrook RUC station and explained who I was saying that I had heard there had been an explosion up there and that policemen had been killed and could they give me any information on who they might be. The officer said, 'hold on until I find out.' He came back in a few minutes and said, 'I'm sorry to tell you that Allen is one of the fatalities.' So with that the two women went hysterical and I tried to calm them down as best I could, and found someone to stay with them until I went to the doctor to get him to come up right away. The doctor came and gave the two women, Allen's wife and my wife injections to calm them down. I then began to phone round the rest of the family, some of them by this time had already heard and had started to gather at the house. Neighbours too had begun to hear and people started to stream to the house to offer sympathy and support. How I learned of my son's death was not very nice, but I had to know.

The irony of Allen's death was that he was not scheduled for duty that day but had agreed to do a colleague's shift.

Allen was one of four police officers based at Bessbrook RUC station killed by a massive IRA bomb near Camlough. All four were patrolling in a police Land Rover when explosives packed into a Ford Transit van was detonated as they passed by on the Millvale Road. Noel Webb, Paul Gray and Robert Lockhart were the other RUC men killed in the explosion.

A LEGACY OF TEARS

The force of the explosion blew the Land Rover to pieces. Other police officers following in another police vehicle said that the Land Rover literally disappeared. The bodies of the four RUC men were so badly mutilated by the explosion that they could only be identified by fingerprints:

> Knowing how they were killed, you know of course what we got home here. Eventually they sent a coffin with what they thought was the remains of Allen Baird. The families of the other policemen killed had the same experience and suffered the same as us. Yet those who carried out these atrocities continued to walk free, planning who was next.

> It was hard to take that they got no sentence for their evil deeds, but our son got sentenced to eternity for simply doing his duty so that others could sleep in their beds at night with a measure of peace and security.

The funeral service was held in St. Matthews Parish Church in Scarva where his father Leslie had been the sexton for many years. The funeral service was conducted by the Rector of Scarva Parish Church, the Rev Andrews, and assisted by the Bishop of Down and Dromore, the Rev George Quinn.

The funeral was a full police funeral led by the RUC band. The whole village was filled with mourners and a lorry load of wreaths expressed sympathies from the vast number of people who specially mourned Allen's death:

> From then on life was difficult. It left a very heavy strain on our lives. My wife, Allen's mother, just went down and down in terms of health. She turned grey in a matter of months, the whole impact of Allen's death was just too much for her to bear.

Our lives were dealt an indelible blow. We will never forget it. We had to try and go on the best we could with our lives, but it wasn't easy. You were always expecting him to come through the door. We saw his children every day living without their Daddy. That was very painful. We could not really get it into our heads that he was really gone and that we would never see him again. You were always thinking that in a few minutes he'd call in, looking for something or looking to know something. After all he lived beside us, we saw him every day, he was in and out all the time and we missed him all the more. It was so hard to take that we would never see him again. It was all the more compounded because we never did get to see him even as a corpse. To really say goodbye.

The doctors in Gilford and the minister in the church were very supportive as was the RUC. The minister came here quite a lot. An RUC woman stayed with us throughout the wake.

Allen's children were only seven and three years old at the time. His daughter Judith does not remember her daddy. His son Gordon remembers him quite well and had to go through life without his daddy. As a result he 'stuck' more closely to us his grandparents. We had to help compensate for the loss of his daddy, as did his other grandparents. I suppose there was some mutual comfort in this.

Those two children grew up without a father; there was no money to educate them. The boy - his ambition was to be a music teacher. He went to music lessons and got all his exams. He then wanted to go to University; the family had to borrow money to pay for his education. However he did qualify and his first job was in a school on the Falls Road, Belfast. Some of the staff and pupils didn't take too kindly to him because he was a Protestant but he stuck it out and stated his case and when he left just over a year ago they did not want him to leave. He now has a teaching post in Italy. Judith too has done well and has held several good jobs.

Allen's youngest brother Wesley did not do well and struggled to concentrate at school after his brother's murder. Noel, another brother, joined the RUC in direct response to the murder of his brother Allen.

To this day, Allen's mother, Mrs Baird wakens many nights with thoughts of Allen, recalling childhood memories of her precious son, how he met his death, her heart breaking and tears flowing. His father, too, says that many a time he wakens thinking, 'have I been dreaming all along, has it all been just a bad dream and then it strikes at your heart that it is not a dream, its all true.'

> I certainly wont be forgiving them. Live and let live is our motto. We have nothing against Roman Catholics but we are very bitter against those who murdered our son, who sat and watched for that Land Rover and pressed the button with the evil intent to kill its occupants.

The family feel that their grief and pain has been compounded by the government's decision to destroy the RUC, disbanded to appease the very republicans who had murdered hundreds of its brave and gallant men. The family feel that the removal of the RUC band from the PSNI added insult to injury.

Commenting on the RUC Leslie Baird said:

> One of the finest forces that ever was. One that any other country would have been proud of. What did my son give his

life for? The RUC were good enough to serve but the government decided that they were not good enough to remain once they had achieved their purpose. All for what? Look at the situation now.

All the symbols we hold dear are being scrapped to appease the IRA. The republicans who carried out this murderous campaign against the decent law abiding citizens of this country have all have been set free and members of their organisation, IRA/Sinn Fein, given positions of power in the government. The IRA men on the run are coming home. My son who gave everything to protect ordinary people in this country is never coming home.

The Group has provided great help and support and we are very thankful for it and we are looking forward to having our 'Memorial Garden'.

In July 1980 Allen Baird's son together with the son of another murdered policeman, Sergeant James Hunter, unveiled a memorial plaque to their murdered fathers on the green in Scarva which is overlooked from the Baird family home across the street. Two months later in September a plaque in memory of the two murdered policemen was also dedicated in St. Matthews Parish Church in Scarva.

I conclude this chapter with a few verses from a poem written by Allen's sister Pauline:

> We live in Northern Ireland,
> With troubles, tears and strife,
> Where so many hearts are broken,
> And so many have lost their life.

A LEGACY OF TEARS

For over thirty years now,
We have had this cross to bear,
Not one person out there,
Even seemed to care.

There was no one there to counsel us,
Or help us through these times,
We had to get on with life,
With it rolling round our mind.

Funeral of Allen Baird

Iris Farley

Desmond Farley is a dairy farmer from outside Markethill, where his family have lived and farmed for generations. Desmond was also a part time member of the UDR for eighteen years having previously served on the 'B' Specials for four years before they were disbanded.

Desmond tells how their lives were first disrupted by a gun attack in January 1976 when three gunmen fired forty-six rounds of ammunition into the home where they were living at the time which was a short distance from the family farm.

Despite the intensity of this attack with several bullets penetrating the windows and doors of their home, amazingly no one was injured.

Desmond and his wife however continued to live under fear of attack as the semi -isolated position of their farmhouse left them vulnerable, particularly when Desmond was coming home from duty with the UDR.

Then in June 1986 RUC Special Branch uncovered a specific threat against Desmond Farley and informed him that his life was in danger.

Desmond remembers how two weeks before he was warned about the threat upon his life, he had been visited by two men whom he did not know, offering to do building work on the farm and who then took off as suddenly as they had appeared. Mr Farley later identified one of the men from security force records as an 'on the run' (OTR) terrorist, suspected of killing a member of the UDR.

Over the next six months the family lived their lives under constant fear. Desmond says: 'We were continually watching out as we went about our daily lives, the whole family felt vulnerable.' Desmond further recalls how over those months his elderly mother would stand in the kitchen with the lights out and watch the lighted yard as he milked the cows each evening: 'What she was going to do if someone appeared I don't know, but she did that anyhow without fail.'

This situation continued until the 1 January 1987 when at about 8.15 pm, their lives were to be shattered, when a lone gunman ran around the side of the house and opened fire hitting Desmond in the arm and leg and fatally wounding his mother.

Desmond takes up the story:

My brother George who had been visiting for New Year was leaving and he had in the car a bag of potatoes that a friend had given him for us at Christmas. He took the bag of potatoes from the car and showed them to me – a lovely bag of pink potatoes. He had just shut the door of the car to drive off, when the 'boy' ran around the corner of the house and fired. I was hit a couple of times in the arm and the leg and my mother was badly wounded as she stood on the doorstep waving goodbye. My brother then pushed my son who was just eight years old in through the door into the house and shouted for me to get in. I was a bit dazed and managed to stagger into the house and lock the door, with my mother still lying outside at the side of the door groaning. We could not do anything as the gunman was still outside. My brother said, 'where's mother?' I said she was lying outside and he said come on and get her in. When we where just about three feet from the door we saw the door handle move, it was the 'boy' trying to open the door to get in. When he couldn't get it opened he fired a burst through the door. We stood aside until he finished. My wife had gone down to the bathroom and put the flare off and the 'boy' vanished. So we went out and carried my mother in and waited for the ambulance.

Desmond and his mother travelled down to hospital in the same ambulance holding each other's hand as they journeyed to hospitals in Belfast. Desmond was taken to Musgrave Park Hospital and his mother to the Royal Victoria Hospital.

Mrs Margaret Iris Farley, whose artery had been severed by a bullet causing severe loss of blood, lost her fight for life and died five weeks later in hospital as a result of her injuries. She was aged seventy years.

Mrs Farley was, 'a devoted parent and sincere Christian who loved her church. Her kind and pleasant nature could not be over emphasised.' She was a home loving woman who loved her family and her grandchildren. Her home was a welcoming home to all.

Desmond's children (aged six and eight at the time) with whom Mrs Farley lived at the family home loved her greatly and would run to granny to be 'rescued' when they were 'in trouble' with mum. Mrs Farley taught them the Word of God, which she loved dearly and at a local Holiday Bible Club a leader had remarked that of all the children attending the Holiday Bible Club nobody knew the Scriptures like the Farley kids.

At her funeral service the local minister, the Rev Edward Smyth, of Redrock Presbyterian Church, where Mrs Farley was a committed member, described her as 'a woman full of hope.' During all her time in hospital despite all of the pain she would say, 'God is good' quoting from her favourite Psalm.

Desmond was released from hospital just the day before his mother died and had been brought across under a 'military operation' from the 'Musgrave' on two occasions to see his mother who was concerned for how he was. Desmond and his brother George were both with their mother when she died.

To add to the family's suffering there was a bomb scare at the farm on the day following the shooting and the family had to be evacuated from their home for twenty-four hours.

Life was not easy for the family following the shooting. Desmond's wife, Margaret, had to try and keep things going as 'normal'. With both her husband and mother-in-law in hospital she had to organise getting the children to and from school and looked after while she visited her husband in the Musgrave hospital and 'granny' in the

Royal hospital. The children were 'flung' from one home to another. Different people stayed at the farm with her each night. Margaret relates that life was awful and without the help of family, friends and neighbours does not know how she could ever have coped.

Family life was not only shattered by the incident that claimed the life of Mrs Farley but totally disrupted.

The family had to try and come to terms with their tragic loss; the grief was compounded for Desmond by the fact that his mother had been murdered in an attempt on his life.

Besides the great pain of their grief was the whole disruption to family life. Their son aged eight had witnessed the gun attack and his granny lying wounded at the door of their home. On that night he and his sister aged six were found standing in the hall of their home hugging each other.

The incident affected their daughter physically, her education too was affected with her progress hampered in the early years following the shooting. To this day when she comes into the house she asks, 'Where's daddy?'

Desmond was medically discharged from the UDR and was unable to work on the farm for two years and had to employ a man to run the farm until he was gradually able to come back to work himself.

There was immense pressure from senior security personnel for the family to move out of their home permanently. For several weeks their home was under permanent guard by the security forces, at times they were escorted to places and the family had to try and cope with the continual fear of living under the constant threat of further repeat attempts on their lives – always looking over their shoulders as they came and went to and from their home in the course of their ordinary every day lives.

The family did consider relocating and viewed other farm properties but since that would have involved leaving the home and farm that had been in the Farley name for generations they decided to stay.

The family did not receive any professional help or counselling and felt that to a large extent they were left to cope alone.

The effects of this brutal murder still live with the family. The impact of the shooting and the murder of Desmond's mother was physically and emotionally enormous. While the family have learned to adapt and get on with their lives, there remains an aching void in their hearts and the vivid memories of the events of that night are forever etched upon their minds. In the outside kitchen wall one bullet hole from the attack remains as a visible reminder of that horrific New Year's night in 1987 when an INLA gunman with his evil heart intent on murder came to their home and gunned down a godly Christian women.

No one was ever arrested or charged in connection with the incident.

The remarkable courage and bravery of this family stands in contrast to the evil and wickedness of that INLA gunman. The family, though deeply scared by the event have been enabled to triumph with steadfastness and faith over the evil that was perpetrated against them, leaving the justice that has been denied them to, 'God the righteous Judge of all the earth who will do right.'

Michael Frederick Leslie Marshall

Pearl and Greer Marshall lived in Glenanne, South Armagh with their three boys Michael, Phillip and Glenn. Michael was their first child, 'our first special baby son' who was born on Thursday 9 July 1964 at the Carleton Maternity Home, Portadown.

Michael grew up with his two brothers in a very happy and secure family environment:

> We all played and laughed together and when the boys needed help. Greer and I were always there for them. Life was good in those days, untouched by evil designs. The Troubles in Northern Ireland were developing, but at least our family remained happy and intact.

Michael went to school in Mountnorris. He was a happy and lively child who loved fun and games with other children: 'He was full of life and was the joy of our hearts.'

The family later moved to Enniskillen in county Fermanagh where Michael attended the Model School and Enniskillen High School. Michael loved sports and was also an enthusiastic member of the Boy Scouts.

In 1976 the family returned to South Armagh, to their home town of Markethill. Michael transferred to Markethill High School and became an avid member of the local football team: 'Football was his life at this point as he grew up into a handsome fine young man.'

Michael later attended Armagh College of Further Education and the Government Training Centre at Craigavon, where he trained as an electrician and took up an apprenticeship with Doak's of Gilford.

In 1982 at eighteen years of age Michael joined the RUC Reserve and was stationed in Carrickmore, County Tyrone for one and a half years. Subsequently he joined the RUC regular force and was stationed in Strandtown in East Belfast. At this time he met and married Donna Whiteside, a girl from Markethill. They set up home in Lisburn. However since Michael was a real home bird, he asked to be transferred back to county Armagh. He was accepted into traffic branch and was stationed in Mahon Road, Portadown, and Michael and his wife came back to live in Markethill just a few doors away from Michael's parents in Mowhan Court:

> Every one was delighted that Michael and Donna were living among their family and friends again, and our joy was complete

with the arrival of their beautiful baby daughter, Michelle. Sadly, however, this happy family circle was soon to be shattered forever. Evil people were planning murder and destruction.

Michael was transferred to the RUC border station of Bessbrook in South Armagh in 1987. Life was dangerous for the brave men and women of the RUC in this particular area. The Bessbrook RUC station bore the brunt of the IRA's evil onslaught in South Armagh. The members of the RUC daily risked their lives to guard a community being held to ransom by terrorists. Many of these brave men and women gave their lives for their country.

However, without the sacrifice of the security forces and their families, no one would have had a moments peace during the years of the Troubles and terrorists would have had a free rein to carry out their evil activities: 'Our son Michael was to be one of those called to make the supreme sacrifice, to lay down his life for the sake of others.'

Mrs Marshall related her memories of the night when her precious first-born son died at the hands of terrorists:

> We shall never forget Friday 20 October 1989. To everyone else this was probably just another day, but the sad events of that Friday are etched on my heart forever. That evening our eldest son was parted from us forever in this life. Who has the right to do such a thing? No one. God gives life, and only He has the right to take it away.
>
> That evening Michael came up to visit us about seven o'clock before he would go on duty at 11pm. Michael was in and out of our home at some time most days. We were all living under the most dreadful strain and threat. At this particular period of the

Troubles there was a very heavy threat on the security forces, so Michael carried his shotgun with him, but he always felt safe when he arrived at his place of work. I remember well my last words to him as he left our home that evening: 'be careful, watch yourself.' Little did we know that would be the last time we would see or hear our son again. Why? For trying to keep the peace.

That night Michael was on duty with another very young policeman who had only been in the RUC for nine months. The two of them were alone in an armoured police-car, travelling towards Belleek, South Armagh. As the two young men approached the village, they came under attack from heavy calibre gunfire. The gunfire was aimed at the engine, stopping it in its tracks. Michael was aware that they were being ambushed. He radioed back to base, 'Attack. Under attack.'

How difficult this is for me, his mother who gave him life, to picture this scene as that very life was cut so short by evil, evil men. This is against nature and all that is good in humanity. This is a crime against heaven itself. No mercy was shown. By this time the car had stopped and as Michael bravely tried to do what he could in the awful circumstances, he struggled with the key and gear lever as the two young men came under continued gunfire. Michael had been shot and it is only with many tears and much anguish that I now record on paper that his short life was over and our beloved son was dead. This is a fact, but it is unfinished business, for our lives are so entirely different now. Part of us died that day, and only those who have endured such an experience, can empathise and truly understand. We would not wish any other human being to share this experience, but so many in Ulster know exactly what we mean.

During this cowardly attack on the two young policemen, in which their vehicle was hit sixty-six times, Michael's colleague's door had opened and though he had multiple gunshot wounds he had crawled out as far as he could. At this stage the car had burst into flames. A passing motorist stopped and pulled the other constable to safety, but there was nothing he could do for Michael – it was too late.

The Marshall family had gone to bed when at 1.05 am came the knock on their door:

> I remember it like yesterday. Time seemed to stand still. I opened our bedroom window and asked who it was. When he said his name I knew immediately something was wrong because I recognised him as a policeman stationed at Bessbrook along with Michael. I knew. I said to him, 'It's Michael.' He said 'Yes'. I said, 'He's dead.' And his reply was 'Yes.' Part of us died too.

Michael Marshall had been cruelly slaughtered by the IRA aged just twenty-five and became the 265th member of the RUC to be killed in the Troubles.

Greer and Pearl had the awful task of going to tell his wife Donna the terrible news that Michael had been murdered, leaving her widowed and his two daughters Michelle (two and a half) and Maxine (nine) orphaned. After that people began to arrive at their home to offer sympathy and support.

The whole community was stunned and shocked. Over the weekend hundreds of people came to the house to pay their respects to a wonderful son.

A LEGACY OF TEARS

The funeral was held on Monday, 23 October 1989 and this was Michael's maternal granny's seventieth birthday. Michael was very fond of his granny and visited her three or four times every week. The streets of Markethill were lined with thousands of mourners; the whole town came to a standstill. The whole community felt the pain. Michael was given a full RUC funeral led by the RUC band as the cortege left Michael's home and proceeded respectfully to St. John's Parish Church, Mullabrack.

Archbishop Robin Eames of Armagh and the Rev Raymond Ferguson, Rector of Mullabrack, conducted the service. The mourners who lined the streets looked on with sadness and solemnity as the RUC band played the Death March. There was a sense of numbness and disbelief among the mourners at the premature death of this young twenty five year old family man so much loved by his family and friends.

In his address at the funeral service, Archbishop Robin Eames described Michael as, 'characteristic of a generation of police officers whose career has been dominated by the struggle against terrorism.' He told mourners: 'When we eventually find peace in Northern Ireland, it will be the Michael Marshalls of this world who will have helped to lay the framework by service, dedication and example that will make it all possible.' Michael's own minister, the Rev Ferguson, described the murder as, 'an act of barbarism' and said that: 'Constable Marshall was dedicated to his work in serving with the RUC. He was also a wonderful family man since his marriage five years ago.'

After the funeral service, Michael was laid to rest in the churchyard of Mullabrack:

> Twenty-five years of joy in that young life were lost to Greer and me forever. He had much living still to do. It is now our

> memories of Michael and the love we shared as a family that
> help us to continue.

Michael was a very sociable and outgoing young man. He was studying for his sergeant's examination at the time he was murdered. He was a member of Redrock Orange Lodge and Markethill Arch Purple as well as Markethill Apprentice Boys. Helping and supporting other people mattered to him and he liked being involved in his local community, where he had many friends. The esteem in which Michael was held by all who knew him, is reflected in the many memorials erected in his memory.

Redrock Orange Lodge erected a memorial stone in their hall in memory of Michael. Markethill Apprentice Boys also put a memorial stone in the Orange hall in Markethill. Markethill Orange District erected a memorial in the square in Markethill with all the names of the murdered Brethren carved in stone. Michael's name is also on the Roll of Honour in Enniskillen High School.

One year on from his murder, on 22 October 1990, in Chapel of Ease Church of Ireland, Markethill, a memorial window displaying the RUC crest was dedicated to Michael.

The family also gave a Cup in memory of Michael to the local High School that Michael had attended to be presented annually to the student who has excelled at sport.

For months people came and visited the family. Sympathy cards arrived in their hundreds, all preserved and perused from time to time. For weeks after Michael's murder neither Pearl nor Greer were able to return to work as a result of all the stress and strain and shock they were suffering:

Family and friends came and went, but at night we were still left alone with our memories and all the unanswered questions. Why had Michael lost his life at the hands of the IRA leaving his wife Donna, his young daughters Michelle and Maxine, his brothers, parents, grandparents and all the wider family circle to pick up the pieces of our lives, so brutally destroyed by the acts of evil men? The effects on a family radiate outwards from the centre, rather like the effects of a stone being dropped into a pool, with the circle spreading outwards ever wider. Each individual family member endures their own grief and suffering. Not one is left untouched by such a tragedy as murder.

After Michael's murder we felt that our lives were in tatters. We felt that nobody cared. People seemed to be getting on with their own lives. We felt so alone. Clergymen, politicians, businessmen and even our own extended family didn't really understand our tremendous loss and how we were coping with it. How we wish Michael had not been murdered.

At the inquest into Michael's murder almost two years later in August 1991 the horrific circumstances by which Michael met his death at the hands of terrorists were recounted to the family who gathered. Michael could only be identified through his dental records.

I can assure you that no one with any human decency would wish what happened to our son ever to happen again. We were left with nothing. Why does God allow such evil deeds to take place?

The family had not only to rebuild their lives but also their homes which were destroyed on two occasions by massive IRA car bombs left near to their homes. One bomb was left just a few days after

Michael's inquest, substantially damaging both homes. Donna did not return to her home after this attack and moved with her daughters to live in Banbridge some twelve miles away in an attempt to make a new start for her and the girls.

Greer and Pearl visit Michael's grave every week, placing fresh flowers on it:

> Each flower is placed with love and wishing Michael was with us to share all the joy we have with the rest of the family members. We find life without him terrible, especially at times like Christmas, birthdays, holidays, and especially at the confirmation of his daughter Michelle.

As I conducted the interview with Pearl I learned that in a few days time it would have been Michael's fortieth birthday. I could feel the pain and the poignancy of that impending date upon Michael's mum as choking back the tears she said:

> We would have been having a big surprise family celebration, but now all I can do is put new flowers on his grave.

> Greer and I and indeed all our family are serving a painful sort of life sentence, deprived of the one we love. This can never change. We think about him every day – when we waken and when we go to bed as well as many times throughout the day. No one has ever been convicted of our son's murder. We cannot and will never forgive those evil men who murdered our son and who show no remorse for their wicked crime. Bitterness did eat us up for a long time, but we have come to realise that life was for living and we are trying to move forward in our lives helping to bring comfort and support to other people in similar situations to ourselves.

A LEGACY OF TEARS

We know for sure that we would prefer to be the parents of the murdered, than to be the parents of the murderers.

Funeral of Michael Marshall

Roger Love

Roger James Love was born on 10 February 1971. This was the beginning of a wonderful relationship between Roger and his mother, Lorna Kelly. Roger was seriously ill at birth and it was three weeks later before this beautiful little baby boy came home.

The family lived in the Killicomaine area of Portadown where Roger grew up attending Killicomaine Junior High School and then the Portadown Technical College. From there Roger went on to Craigavon Training Centre and achieved a City in Guilds in a number of skills. He took up employment in the 'Mayfair' factory but his goal was to be a policeman like his maternal grandfather. He enrolled in the TA and joined the TA band as a left-handed drummer. Later he made application to the RUC and was informed that recruitment at that particular time was not open to his age and to apply again in two years. Undeterred and against his parents wishes Roger applied to the Armagh Battalion of the UDR.

Roger was delighted when in October 1990 he was accepted into the UDR and a colleague at the 'Mayfair' who was also a part time UDR man gave him a pen which he treasured and carried with him wherever he went. Soon after his UDR passing out parade Roger bought himself a new car, a Vauxhall Nova which was his pride and joy:

> Roger was such a happy, good-looking young man, he loved people, and people loved him. He had a great big smile and everybody he met spoke of his lovely smile, his lovely eyes and white teeth. Roger lived and enjoyed life to the full. You could not dislike him. He and I were especially close, we had a special bond. I think it was partly because for the first three weeks of his life I didn't know if he was going to survive or not and partly because I was a young mother of just 19 years when Roger was born. We were best friends.

When Roger joined the UDR he was living with his mother and sister Julianne in Sleepy Valley, Richhill.

In January 1990 Roger's mother, Lorna, had a baby girl Carolyn. Later in the year a third daughter, Laura, was born. When Roger accompanied his mother to register the baby's birth, staff took him for the father: 'We had such a laugh at this. Roger loved his baby sisters Carolyn and Laura and often took Carolyn with him in his car.'

Roger had being going out with a girl Sharon for about a year and they decided to get engaged planning to be married the following year on Sharon's birthday in July 1991. On his twentieth birthday family and friends had gone out for a meal. It was such a happy occasion; friends from across the religious divide were there: 'Roger made no difference. His best friend was a Catholic and Roger had been attacked and given a broken nose because of this friendship. But Roger was determined that he would not allow that to affect his friendship.'

Roger was in the prime of life. Life was good and Roger was very happy. He was surrounded with love and had so much love to give. He loved his job and he took great pride in the UDR, always doing his own uniform and gave himself wholly to the job which he was doing. The UDR meant everything to him. One of his senior officers had said that Roger would go far in the UDR. He was teased because he had the biggest head in the Regiment - that is cap size!

In the midst of this happy environment, there was a little incident when a bird hit the kitchen window in their house. Roger took this as an omen from an 'old wives tale' that someone was going to die. The next week he brought home forms to record next of kin: 'He seemed to be convinced that he was going to die, that he was going to be killed.'

> On the 1 March 1991, Roger was due to start work at 2pm. We had a lovely morning together. I had made him breakfast he walked down to the shop to get the local paper, the Portadown Times, and then I made him his favourite dinner, 'mince and onions'. Roger thanked me and asked if I wanted a lift into the village to do messages, I said no and he kissed me goodbye and said that he might be late home and not to worry. Roger then left to see Sharon before he would go on duty.

Lorna's husband Keith also worked part time in the UDR. He was also on duty that day. His task was to supply the 'men' with food.

Lorna recalled how that evening she bathed Carolyn and Laura and put them to bed and then washed her hair around 9pm. Just at that time a neighbour came to the door to tell her that a bomb had exploded in Armagh:

> We had no phone in the house, but I thought Keith will be okay he was just taking food to the men. I never thought at that moment that it could be Roger. Then it dawned on me what if it is Roger and I got down on my knees and prayed to God 'please don't let it be Roger or Keith.' I listened to the 10 o'clock news which was just a simple report with little detail. The neighbour tried to phone through to the camp but could not get through. The next bulletin said that there had been an incident on the Killylea Road, Armagh and I really started to worry but kept trying to convince myself that they were both all right.
>
> At around 11pm I heard what I knew to be Keith's car coming down 'Sleepy Valley'. When he arrived my sister in law was with him. I ran down the stairs and opened the door. I thought it's Roger he's dead. The news was that he had been seriously injured and had been taken to Craigavon hospital for emergency surgery.

Roger was part of a two-vehicle patrol driving towards Armagh city along the Killylea Road shortly before 9pm. As the patrol moved off from temporary traffic lights at road works a massive rocket exploded at the rear of the first vehicle with devastating consequences. Private Paul Sutcliffe aged thirty-two died instantly at the scene. Roger was to die later from his injuries and two other UDR men were also seriously injured in the cowardly and savage attack by the IRA.

Following the news Lorna and her husband Keith rushed to Craigavon hospital:

A LEGACY OF TEARS

My sister came with me and as we were sitting in the quiet of the relative's room another of my sisters came screaming across the hospital car park. At around 3am medical staff informed us that Roger had undergone emergency surgery, was on a life support machine and was now being transferred to the Royal Victoria hospital in Belfast. They said his condition was serious but 'stable' though he would not be able to speak for a week.

I was allowed to see him briefly, I could hardly recognise him. His face was covered in cuts and his head bandaged and his tongue hanging out. The only place I could kiss him was on his nose. It was unreal, it seemed like slow motion, this could not be my child.

I wanted so desperately to go with him in the ambulance. I thought if he is going to die I want, I need to be with him. It was not possible for me to go with him and I was reluctantly persuaded to go home to my two babies. But I could not settle at home. I phoned the Royal and spoke to a Sister O'Neill and asked if I could go down and see my son.

The answer was 'yes of course' and I made my way immediately down to the Royal. When Roger came out of surgery at the Royal he looked much better though he had various serious wounds and was on a life support machine.

I sat and held his hand and talked to him until 6am leaving the ward periodically to allow medical staff to attend to him. The Rev Knowles arrived and prayed with us. Then Roger's dad arrived and we both stayed all day Saturday. Newsrooms phoned the hospital for regular reports on his condition.

I phoned home to inquire about the babies, the family encouraged, coaxed me to go home and eventually I did. I saw my two babies, I tried to sleep but couldn't, then the Royal phoned to ask us to come down immediately. At the Royal we were met by a doctor who with tears told us that Roger was brain dead. I asked to see him. Then he was taken to have tests carried out to confirm his condition as 'brain dead' that took all day Sunday. The doctors then asked if we would donate his organs. I couldn't bear that thought on top of all that he had gone through, but because he was going to have to undergo a post mortem and because I knew it is what Roger would have wanted, I with his father reluctantly agreed.

As a result of his injuries only the kidneys were able to be donated. Roger was transferred to the Belfast City Hospital for the removal of his organs and it was Wednesday before the body was returned home.

One of the recipients of Roger's kidneys was a man celebrating his twenty fifth wedding anniversary from whom Lorna received a lovely letter thanking her for the 'gift of life' that he had received through the tragic loss of her son.

The family now had to plan for the funeral of Roger.

The Rev Knowles arrived and prayed with me and Roger's fiancée Sharon. We found ourselves making arrangements for the funeral. I wanted Roger buried beside his maternal grandmother in Seagoe Cemetery, Portadown and in full dress uniform of the UDR.

The funeral service was held in Edenderry Presbyterian Church conducted by the Rev Knowles who said that Roger was: 'A very kind and generous and happy and outgoing young lad who enjoyed life, and whose murder, was yet another pointless death.' The Rev

Knowles added: 'This war is not a war against the men folk in our community but against wives, children, parents and grandparents; they are left with years of aching empty broken hearts.' He continued, 'But the terrorists will stop. Sooner or later they will die and stand before God in judgement. No murderer has eternal life abiding in him.'

Taking part in the funeral service was former Moderator of the Presbyterian Church, Dr James Matthews, who said the murder was an, 'evil, cowardly and outrageous act' and added: 'May I remind those who committed it that their crime, in the final analysis, was committed not just against the four UDR men but against God who created them and us.'

> I was amazed at the support but as everyone left the cemetery at Seagoe and I was driven off it was the worst moment of my life.

The neighbours in Sleepy Valley were a great support; Lorna described them as, 'amazing especially Dorothy Corkin.'

For most of the period since Roger's death Lorna had not seen her two babies who were being cared for by relatives. On returning to the house after the funeral Lorna asked for the babies to be brought back home, 'I just sat and cried.'

In all of this, Lorna's older daughter, Julianne, just fifteen years old had in many ways been forgotten: 'I had been caught up in my own grief but Keith my husband was a rock. He was just wonderful with Julianne who was grieving deeply for her brother.'

> I needed space to grieve but there was no space. I had two young babies, Carolyn and Laura, who needed to be looked after. They needed me. I would say that if it had not been for the babies

keeping me going I would probably have taken a breakdown.

I talked incessantly about Roger, I would tell everyone how wonderful he was and how he was murdered by the IRA.

I joined the UDR widows and mothers group. Reatha Hassan was a great help and I made many good friends through the Group who had come through similar experiences especially those widows of the Glenanne UDR base bombing. There was an 'empathy' between us and we shared our feelings and talked about our loved ones.

Despite the intensity of Lorna's grief and loss she realised just two years ago that in many ways she had not really grieved and that she needed help:

I was still talking incessantly about Roger and it was as if to me he was still alive, I had not let go. I was unable to do normal everyday things. I was unable to look after the finances of the house. I attended counselling with Cruise for eighteen months this really helped me to move on and to stop talking always about Roger and helped control the anger I felt at what had happened to Roger.

I do still feel angry against those who killed Roger. I don't call them terrorists. They are just evil men who had no justification for what they did to my only son. They robbed me of a lovely boy and his murder did not advance their cause one bit. I will never know what it would have been like to see his children and watch them grow up. I am not a bitter person. I grew up in a mixed area of Portadown and I knew and had many Roman Catholic friends. It hurt me that some of them changed their attitude towards me and have never yet said to me about what happened to Roger. I have also protected my girls from the full horror of what happened to Roger, they have never been shown the memorial album. I did not want them to grow up with prejudice or bitterness towards Roman Catholics.

I have not forgiven those who murdered Roger because they have never repented of their evil or sought my forgiveness with remorse. I can't understand people who say they can just forgive someone who murdered their loved ones. I have to leave it with God for He said, 'vengeance is mine I will repay.' These people will have to stand before God.

Through this bitter experience, five years after Roger's death I came to know Jesus Christ as my Saviour and that has been a great help to me in recent years. I am beginning to move on. He is changing me and some of my attitudes but I do still hurt and I still come home at times and just sit and cry. I still miss Roger so much but I know that I will see him again one day.

I still think about him every day and often come home and cry. It's hard to take in.

Life has and never will be the same again for Lorna since the loss of her son Roger. Her health has been affected and her whole life devastated by this senseless barbaric act. One of the ironies in this tragedy was that when Roger would have come off duty that night, he was due to go on two weeks leave, which was marked in his diary that we leafed through.

As I listened to Lorna's story, and turned through the pages of the memorial photo album to Roger, I was deeply moved. I observed yet another mother with deep heartfelt grief for her murdered son that will not be healed until God wipes away all tears from her eyes on that great day when she enters His presence. Yet I observed a woman of remarkable strength of character that stands in stark contrast to the cowardly evil men who murdered her son Roger.

Today a memorial to Roger and others from the village who lost their lives in the Troubles stands in Roger's county Armagh home village of Richhill.

I close the story with one of the many tributes paid to Roger after his death: 'A young man who brought the sun into everyone's day. Remembered with love.'

Funeral of Roger Love

Robert (Bobby) Crozier

Bobby Crozier who was an only child, lived with his wife Agnes and two daughters Roberta and Davina in their home at 21 Ashlea Bend, Markethill.

As I spoke to his wife Agnes and daughter Roberta it was very apparent that Bobby Crozier was one of this world's true gentlemen. He was a man who loved his wife and who was absolutely devoted to his two 'girls'.

Bobby worked in the local Spence Bryson factory as a linen dresser and served part time on the UDR. Like so many other men on the UDR he had first served on the 'B' Specials. His daughter Roberta spoke of growing up from her late primary school days with a very real sense of pride in what her Dad did although always conscious that she could not really speak to anyone about his 'job' in the UDR. For her it was a very important job and she was aware at first that there was some kind of 'risk' involved, becoming more conscious of that risk and its impact upon their lives as teenagers.

On a couple of occasions the town of Markethill itself was bombed and living right on the edge of town the impact of those bombs instilled a sense of fear. Roberta recalls how, throughout those days when almost on a daily basis there was news of people in the security forces being murdered, she was affected sub-consciously with thoughts of: 'there's always a chance it could happen to daddy some day' although she coped by thinking, 'well its always somebody else it will never happen to us.'

Daddy was everything that anyone could wish for in a daddy. He was all that a Daddy could be or should be. He would have done anything for us; he worshiped the ground his 'girls' walked on. Always willing to do things for us. Even down to the school sports days when he would take us out to Gosford park and 'train' us, getting us running and jumping. Sometimes he would take us up to the High School sports track to time us running and to practise the long jump. He just wanted the best for us in life and helped us to reach those goals. He always looked after us; he was always there for us. I worked from about the age of eleven in a wee shop around the corner from the house 'Minish's'. It was open late on a Saturday night and Daddy would come round to meet me because even though it was just around the corner he didn't want me walking home on my own. He was very protective of us and went out of his way to look after us and to provide for us as a family. One day while on teaching practice in Bangor High School, waiting for the bus I phoned home and Daddy just insisted that he would come down and pick me up and bring me home. Every time I would phone home from Stranmillis, mum said it was a rush for him to get to the phone first. He was very proud of whatever achievements his girls accomplished at school or wherever. My graduation was a very proud day for him. A man from the town met us in Belfast that day and said he would never forget the perpetual smile that Daddy had on his face. Daddy was a very kind man. It didn't matter who you were – Catholic, Protestant, black or white, he took time to help people.

One particular day he was leaving the house to come and pick us up at Armagh Swimming Pool when he came on a neighbour Catholic women who had fallen and broken her arm and he helped her and wouldn't leave her until the ambulance came. That was the kind of man Daddy was.

The impact on family life with a husband and a father in the security forces was very great although the family were not always conscious of at as they lived through those days. Roberta said:

While you never thought about it at the time, looking back there were many ordinary everyday things that were different because of being a 'security force' family.

For a period of time the two girls had to attend the orthodontist in Newry and travelling to and from Newry was made complicated because of the risk to Bobby. Roberta recounted:

Daddy could only drop us off at the edge of the town and we would have to walk maybe a mile or more into the dentist and out again rain, hail or snow, to a 'safe' place where Daddy would pick us up.

When I learned to drive, Daddy was never keen for me to take the car. I had assumed for most of that time that it was because he was worried about me having an accident, but it was because he always was afraid that while the car was parked somewhere, terrorists might plant a booby trap bomb under it. I had to learn to look under the car even though we had no idea what we were looking for. As a family we could not ever go down South for a day or a holiday. You always had to be careful opening the door, blinds had to be kept closed. It was a terrible way to live your life, although at the time we didn't really think about it growing up. Life for us growing up in Northern Ireland with a member of the family on the security forces could not be described as normal.

Mrs Crozier recalled that:

Life was not easy. When he went out on duty you were worried until you heard the key in the lock in the wee small hours of the morning. There was always that fear, that sense of threat, that worry that they might kidnap him going up the road to Glenanne. Every time you said cheerio you did wonder deep down if you would ever see him again.

Bobby would only have got a few hours sleep until he had to be up for work in the factory. He was a very dedicated soldier. It would have taken a lot for Bobby to miss his duty.

On one occasion the family remember gunfire just a short distance outside the house moments after Bobby had left the house to go and put the car in the garage. Agnes his wife was bathing Davina and left her to run downstairs and outside to see. However it was not Bobby but another sectarian attack on a Catholic man who lived nearby. People actually sent for Bobby to see if he could help with some basic first aid until the ambulance arrived: 'That was Bobby, it didn't matter about religion he was always willing to help others in need.'

Bobby eventually became a full time soldier in the UDR and took up a guard post at the Glenanne base. He held the rank of lance corporal in the 2nd Co. Armagh Battalion

The incident that was to claim Bobby's life happened on 31 May 1991.

Bobby's favourite uncle, Jonny, was in a nursing home in Hamiltonsbawn and was seriously ill. Bobby had sat most of the day with him on the Thursday before his death. He left his uncle Johnny to come home and go on duty. Just before he left for work he received word that his uncle had died. Bobby went on to do his duty, came home on Friday morning and went out to help organise the funeral arrangements, taking no rest or sleep. He helped carry his uncle's remains into the Presbyterian church for the funeral to be held on Saturday. He arrived home shortly after three o'clock in the afternoon and though extremely tired spent the afternoon with the family. He and Agnes covered up vegetables and talked about the holiday that they had arranged to Blackpool. Now that the girls were grown up it was the first time that just the two of them were going on holiday and the girls were staying at home. It was a very happy afternoon. There was a lot of carrying on with the girls. Roberta was going to a band parade in Newtownhamilton and was planning to go to Cranfield the following day with friends.

However Bobby was very tired and his wife had encouraged him to take the night off and stay at home on account of his uncle's death. This was something that she had never done before. Bobby had refused saying that on that night the base was very short of men. He was determined to go on duty. Agnes made the tea. Roberta had burned her hand tonging her hair and Bobby had as always saw to his 'girl' even though she was twenty two. Davina with boyfriend Brian were heading out to a barbeque.

Bobby was picked up by a comrade and went on duty up at Glenanne base, stopping off en route to check if the old Kilcluney graveyard where his uncle was to be buried the next day was tidy. He had said his usual farewell saying, 'I'll see you in the morning.'

Later that night another colleague had tried to persuade Bobby to go home because he had the funeral the next day, but Bobby refused.

Agnes had gone to visit a neighbour, Mrs Adair, and coming home at about 11.00 pm thought she would phone Bobby - something that she would not normally have done. However, as time went on she thought it was getting late and didn't make the call. She went to bed and watched the 'Kelly' show on television. At about 11.20 pm there was an almighty explosion. The loudest bomb they had ever heard. The sound of the bomb was different from any other bomb they had ever heard it seemed to roll across the sky like thunder. So intense was the noise that they thought it was in or around Markethill. The people started to pour out onto the street to see where the bomb had gone off. Everybody was asking, 'where was the bomb?' Agnes had a passing fear that it might be Glenanne then others on the street were shouting, 'maybe it's Glenanne' and fear began to grip the family. Roberta phoned the base to talk to her Daddy, but the phones were dead.

The explosion was caused by a 2500lb IRA bomb packed in a lorry and rolled down a hill into the perimeter fence of the UDR base at Glenanne. The explosion was heard over 50 miles away and devastated the base claiming the lives of three full time UDR men as well as damaging over 50 local houses and killing cattle in a nearby field. A senior fire brigade officer said that the scene was one of, 'utter devastation.'

Lance corporal Bobby Crozier, aged just forty-six, was one of the three full time UDR men killed in this massive bomb attack on the Glenanne UDR base. He died along with his UDR colleagues, Sydney Hamilton and Paul Blakely.

Shortly after the explosion people began to arrive at the Crozier home. Roberta phoned Davina to come home and when she arrived Roberta met her outside and they hugged. Davina ran in to the house and threw herself on the floor screaming 'it's not fair Mummy, it's not fair.' Family began to arrive and cups of tea were made throughout the night, but still nobody told them that Bobby had been killed. Agnes noticed a relative putting up three fingers to someone and thought to herself that he obviously meant that there were three dead. Another neighbour arrived and Agnes knew by the look on her face that she knew more than she was saying. Dr Livingstone arrived and gave her a tablet, then the local Minister, the Rev Ferguson arrived, but still nobody said that Bobby was dead.

Some time later Reatha Hassan who was a family friend and also a UDR Welfare Officer, arrived and informed the family that Bobby was one of those missing and that they should not build up their hopes.

Other people phoned the house throughout the night. One lady whose husband was on duty at Glenanne with Bobby that night phoned several times to see if there was any further news about the causalities. Then eventually on one of these phone calls, Roberta could hear the sense of relief in her voice; she had received news that her husband was alive and well. The lady went on to say that there were three dead and asked Roberta if she wanted her to say who they were. Roberta cannot recall answering the question but was told that her father was one of them. Roberta dropped the receiver and ran out into the garden but never said to any of the rest of them about the phone call.

As the hours slowly passed the family increasingly 'knew' that Bobby was dead. They knew that if alive, somehow he would have got a message to them.

Yet Roberta was still clinging to hope but Agnes felt sure Bobby was never coming home: 'I picked up on expressions from people who came to the house from far and near. I felt that the people in the house knew that Bobby was dead.'

Roberta recalled standing outside that night when a car similar to her Daddy's drove up and she shouted: 'there's my Daddy now, Daddy's here, he's alright, he's alright', but it was not her Daddy. It was a neighbour's grandson. If Roberta had been thinking straight she would have remembered that her father had not taken his car to work that night.

However it was 7.30 am the next morning before the UDR came with 'official' word that Bobby had been killed in the explosion.

Davina stayed in her own room over the whole period of the wake and has never spoken openly about her father's murder.

Catholics and Protestants poured into the house to express their condolences. Letters arrived from all kinds of people - many from Catholic people who felt ashamed that people from their side had done such a thing.

Everybody spoke of Bobby Crozier as a true gentleman. He was involved in the vestry of Kilcluney Parish Church. As a young lad he had been in the Boys Brigade, sang in the church choir and was a member of Redrock Flute Band. He was also a member of Redrock

Orange Lodge, the Royal Black Perceptory and Apprentice Boys.

The funeral was held on Monday 3 June 1991 in St. Johns Parish Church Kilcluney. It was a dignified military funeral. The family were proud of Bobby. He died as a dedicated soldier. Mrs Crozier showed me the long service and good conduct medal that he had received just one month before he was killed.

The funeral service was conducted by Archbishop Robin Eames who conducted the funerals of all three of the murder victims from the Glenanne bomb. Archbishop Eames described the day as one, 'of great sadness for county Armagh.' Speaking at the funeral service of Bobby Crozier the Archbishop said: 'There is a power of evil driving the lives and actions of certain people. These actions have brought misery and suffering to so many. This evil will never conquer us.' Bobby's favourite hymn, 'Will your anchor hold' was sung.

However, not content that they had taken this man's life, the rabid hatred of republicans against the Protestant community was visited on the grieving family by the desecration of the grave on three separate occasions. On the first Remembrance Day a number of poppy wreaths had been placed on the grave as well as a beautiful bunch of red flowers by the family. The next day when they visited the grave everything had been removed, some torn in shreds, others had disappeared altogether. On another occasion flowers and pot were stolen and again the UDR memorial plinth was also removed and later found by the police in 'bandit' country - smashed.

A short time after the funeral, when Roberta had gone to visit the grave and to put on new flowers, a man driving a lorry pulled up alongside her, wound down the window and laughed as loud as he could as she knelt placing flowers on her father's grave:

The physical pain in my chest was immense, which did eventually lift when I went up to Glenanne and walked around the site of the base where Daddy had been killed, but the emotional pain is with us every day.

The impact and effects of Bobby's death were felt especially on occasions like the girls' weddings. Roberta said: 'it was a right that we were denied.' On the birth of the first grandchild, a wee boy, Agnes cried the whole day. Bobby never saw his girls married or his grandchildren born and growing up:

> We have been left with a life sentence of which we have now served thirteen years, but we have our memories and no one can rob us of those great and precious memories of a wonderful man. He would just have loved the wee grandchildren we can just picture him.

> The Rev Ferguson was a 'rock' to the family. He visited us very often. He was always there, by our side at anniversaries, remembrance days and the unveiling of the memorial plaque at Redrock Orange Hall etc. He was a real help. Our faith brought us through, because we knew God was there to help us, God did help us, we got strength from God and our faith and through pastoral care from Rev Ferguson.

> We also drew strength from each other and from knowing that there were others who were thinking about us, many of whom had gone through a similar experience.

> We did get strength and were able to go on with our lives, but our lives did change, there was always that empty chair, the space around the kitchen table. We would have terrible dreams in which Bobby had returned. We think these are the result of the

fact that the coffin was not opened. We were not able to see him and say our farewells. We were denied saying our farewells and it was more difficult to accept that he was gone because he left perfectly well that night and we never got to see him again.

Roberta recalls going secretly into the bedroom and attempting to lift the coffin to 'see' if the coffin was heavy enough to reassure her that there was a body in the coffin. We comforted ourselves about the extent of the injuries by building up a mental picture of just a bump to the head.

The family were not able to have an open coffin due to the severity of Bobby's injuries. The extent of those injuries was not revealed to the family but they were to have the terrible experience of later unexpectedly reading about them in a book, *'Testimony to Courage'*, some ten years later. That horrendous experience traumatised the family immensely, their anguish was uncontrollable with terrible physical and emotional effects upon them all for days and weeks to come. It was as if it had just happened all over again.

Nobody was ever convicted of this murder and the family do feel justifiably angry. As Archbishop Eames said at the funeral service: 'justified anger is not unchristian:'

> We can only look at it that they got off with it in this life but they will be judged for it some day when they meet their Maker. People often ask us do we forgive them, I just answer that by saying its not up to us to forgive them its up to God to forgive them and in a way you have to ask for forgiveness and I don't think those people are going to ask for forgiveness. We are bitter, not towards the ordinary Roman Catholic, but yes to those men who went out to deliberately commit murder. It doesn't matter who they are, that's wrong. It's wrong to kill anybody.

A LEGACY OF TEARS

We try to forget about them. We could be meeting them in the
street. They never were brought to justice, they have got away
with it, and they are walking about free today. They have never
had to answer for what they did. It's the families of the victims
who have been given the life sentence, every day, especially at
birthdays and anniversaries.

We never got any help, as children (over eighteen) we were
forgotten about, apart from our minister there was no
counselling. The 'Group' has helped by meeting with others who
have gone through similar experiences.

Roberta reflected: 'I like to go to the memorial garden at Glenanne
and gather my thoughts.'

Who can ever fully recount the anguish of another life taken,
another family devastated by the brutality of the IRA murderous
campaign? Words cannot ever convey the horror that republicans
inflicted upon this and other families by their evil deeds.

*The scene of devastation at the Glenanne
Army base in South Armagh.*

David Dougan

This brief story has been told by Mrs Dougan following the recent, sudden and tragic death of her husband David. The story reflects something of the tremendous courage of the whole family as they battled to cope with life following the attempt on David's life in 1992.

It was bedtime: around 10.30 pm on Tuesday 9th September 1992 when a gunman fired eight rounds of automatic gunfire at the family home. The noise was absolutely unbelievable, deafening, frightening, it seemed the house was coming down around us. Eventually when the shooting stopped, we were petrified, gasping, reeling with shock, and then to our horror, David was lying on the floor with blood pouring out of him. Seven bullets entered his body some lodging in the body others passing through the body.

A LEGACY OF TEARS

There was complete and utter mayhem, then the ambulance arrived and David was rushed off to hospital at high speed. We looked helplessly on! David was very critically ill. He had received wounds to his bowel, spleen, back and upper arm. He was unconscious and was placed on a life support machine. David remained in this condition for many months. Then after the long hard battle for life the sad news came. He was paralysed from the waist down. Eventually, after almost one year David was able to come home and after many more months of pain and suffering he was able to walk again, albeit on crutches and for short distances.

David suffered great pain throughout the years but always showed tremendous determination and courage and bore his injuries with great fortitude. The family suffered the pain and anguish with him but there was joy too! Joy that David was alive and able to be at home with us! We had lots of support from our family, and friends and we greatly appreciated this.

Then suddenly and sadly as a result of the attack on his life thirteen years ago, David passed away on 13 October 2005. His unexpected and untimely passing left his family, his extended family, his numerous friends and the wider community deeply traumatised and completely devastated. David who was a civilian victim will always be remembered for his wit, his charm, his cheerfulness and his great zest for life. David was a loving and devoted husband and father and we will love and miss him always.

Reatha Hassan OBE

Reatha Hassan was a member of the UDR and served twenty-one and half years in the 2nd Armagh Battalion of the Regiment, eight years as a part time soldier and thirteen years as a full time member.

Reatha was born and reared in the county Armagh town of Markethill and worked initially as a civil servant. After the formation of the UDR in 1972 and the subsequent heavy loss of life within the Province mainly at the hands of republican terrorists during 1972 when 496 people were murdered, (258 civilians and 151 members of the security forces, which included 26 UDR soldiers), it was decided in 1973 to open recruitment to the UDR to women. The 2nd Armagh Battalion was the first to recruit women.

Reatha Hassan, motivated by a desire to serve her country in those dark days of republican terrorism, joined the 2nd Armagh Battalion of the UDR in 1973 as a part time soldier together with five other women. Her duties were similar to that of the men and she recalls doing foot patrol duty two nights per week in those early days as well as vehicle patrols.

Reatha's story is about what she witnessed during her years as a member of the UDR. The horror and extent of the IRA's bloody and murderous campaign and its effect and impact upon the lives of so many decent, ordinary law abiding people simply because they sought to serve their country and protect the lives of their fellow citizens, Roman Catholic and Protestant alike, from the onslaught of terrorist activity, is impossible to convey in any story.

During her years as a member of the UDR, Reatha had sixty-eight colleagues murdered by republicans. Reatha's story focuses on just a few of those incidents, though obviously the total impact of every loss of life and countless injuries sustained by the brave men and women of the UDR have left an indelible mark upon her heart and life.

Reatha recalls the death of the first UDR soldier of the 2nd Armagh Battalion murdered after she joined the Regiment: 'That was young Sidney Watt. Sidney, just thirty-six years old and a part time member of the UDR who was ambushed and murdered outside his home by the IRA on 20 July 1973. It was very sad, he left a young wife and four small children.'

Reatha spoke of how she visited Sidney's wife Florence whom she had known, after the murder of Sidney and witnessed not only the grief, but also the sheer hardship under which the family struggled to survive.

It was realised that to help support the families of UDR personnel who were killed or injured that some kind of benevolent or welfare fund was needed. Major Charlie Armstrong a part time soldier in the UDR who was also later to be murdered by the IRA, was influential in instigating the setting up of the UDR Welfare and Benevolent Fund, though it was the late 1970s before there was a proper 'welfare' for UDR personnel. Reatha related how the Fund developed:

> In the early days every soldier gave one pound when a colleague was murdered to go to help support the widow. When the Benevolent Fund began every soldier gave a small amount each month to the Fund. The contributions gradually increased over the years and eventually by the time I left the UDR the contribution from each member was equivalent to two days pay per year. Numerous fund raising events were also organised by the individual Battalions to help boost the Funds.

Reatha was attached to the 'welfare' side of the UDR although she carried out other duties during her service, vehicle and foot patrols and other roles such as recruitment and held the ranks of company sergeant and major.

Reatha remembers well the murder of the first UDR women soldiers (Greenfinches as they were commonly known) of the 2nd Armagh Battalion. Margaret Hearst aged just twenty-four was murdered on 8 October 1977 by IRA gunmen who burst into her mobile home situated near Tynan. One of the bullets fired by the gunmen actually went through a cuddly toy clutched by her three year old daughter, Crystal, as she lay sleeping in her cot. Gillian Liggett aged thirty-three and married with two children was shot dead in an IRA ambush on the Armagh to Middleton Road on 6 April 1976 while on routine patrol with the UDR. Reatha said that: 'You never thought that the IRA would kill a woman; you used to think that when women were out with a UDR patrol that they were keeping the patrol safe, in that you thought if the IRA saw there were women they would not attack.' Reatha recalled doing a patrol in Crossmaglen when a group of people outside a pub shouted: 'If you have any sense get away from those men.'

The murder of Margaret Hearst and Gillian Liggett served to further demonstrate the callous brutality of the IRA's murderous and evil campaign. The IRA cold bloodedly murdered its victims without distinction of gender and they certainly were no respecter of persons:

> The most difficult and traumatic incidents to deal with as a Welfare Officer were when soldiers were killed on duty and you had to go to the scene or to visit the injured and dying men. You would go to try and comfort them as they came in injured and dying. It was very difficult to see grown men in the state that they were in following an IRA attack.

The most traumatic incident that Reatha encountered was the murder of two colleagues in an IRA ambush on a routine UDR patrol at Killyleagh Road, Armagh on 1 March 1991. Two other UDR soldiers were seriously injured in the attack. Reatha takes up the story:

> I got word about the incident and was told that there had been four serious causalities, one had been taken to the Medical Centre in the Armagh Camp, two to Musgrave Park Hospital in Belfast and another to Craigavon Area Hospital.
>
> On arrival at the Medical Centre I sat in the waiting room for quite a time and eventually asked one of the male nurses why am I sitting here when I'm needed across the way? The nurse

responded by saying that the police were in the Medical Centre
and waiting for the Welfare Officer to come over to identify the
body because they had a soldier in there dead. When the police
officer came out, he said we were expecting the Welfare Officer
to be a man and I said no that I was the Welfare Officer. The
policeman proceeded to ask me if I knew Paul Sutcliffe and I
said yes I knew him very well and I was then asked if I would
come in to identify the body.

An army medical doctor came out wearing a surgical mask and
warned me that the sight was not very pleasant and if I felt that
I couldn't go in or if I went in and felt ill or unable to proceed
just to say. So I said I was all right. I didn't know what I felt. I
was numb and I suppose the adrenalin was high. Despite his
injuries, I recognised that it was Paul and confirmed his identity.
When I left the Medical Centre at that time I could say that it
didn't really seem to affect me all that much.

I was then informed that the Army did not know who was in
Craigavon but I was asked if I would go and see them. At that
point a colleague, Keith Kelly, came over and asked me if I knew
if Roger Love was injured. It didn't register with me at the time,
but this man would have been his stepfather.

I said that I was heading to Craigavon Hospital to see who was
there and that I would like some company if he would like to
come and he agreed and travelled down to Craigavon with me.
On arrival at Craigavon we went into causality and spoke to the
sister in charge saying that we were here to see the soldier that
was injured. The sister's reply was quite abrupt telling me that
it wasn't me he needed to see it was a priest. I replied to her that
if it is who we think it is it's not actually a priest he would need
but if a minister is required we would arrange for a minister to

see him. I then asked if I could see him and she said no we couldn't. So we were still none the wiser as to who the soldier might be. The sister eventually brought out items belonging to the injured soldier which included a slip of paper that had been in his pocket. I recognised it as Army issue and Roger Love's name was on it.

This was a big shock to me. Roger was a young lad who had been in the UDR part time for only about six months and had then decided to join full time. That meant he had to go to the UDR camp at Ballykinler to do his training. Training lasted for a number of months and he had just finished his training a month when he was caught up in this IRA attack on his patrol.

Roger was a good-looking young man, lovely sparkling blue eyes and beautiful teeth; I used to say he was the best advert for Maclean's toothpaste. We left the hospital to locate his mother and break the news to her and bring her down to the hospital.

From Craigavon we travelled on down to Musgrave Park Hospital to see the other two men, both of whom had serious injuries. One had major 'bomb blast' injuries to his body and the other had lost a leg. Although seriously wounded both these men survived.

The two deaths, however took their toll upon Reatha. She was deeply affected by the deaths of these two young colleagues, twenty-four and twenty-one years old respectively, but in many ways seemed to cope and continued to serve with the UDR. Reatha related how it was in more recent years that the whole impact of these two deaths in particular have effected her:

I can remember as well an occasion in the year 2000 when

shopping in Newry for an outfit for going to Buckingham Palace to receive my OBE, when a comment by a shop assistant brought to my mind very vivid images of the scene in the room in the Army Medical Centre Armagh Barracks where I had identified Paul Sutcliffe. For weeks that vision haunted me and I had to receive counselling.

Also, I remember when we were going through one of the outhouses at Bingham House *(premises purchased by the victim's Group SAVER/NAVER of which Reatha is chairperson)* in 2003, when a tube of Macleans toothpaste fell from a shelf and like a flash I could visualise Roger Love.

I think, part of the reason I took Roger's death so badly was that I did a lot to get him accepted into the UDR after he had initially been turned down because of the particular risk where he lived. In some ways I felt responsible for his death.

Another of the major incidents which Reatha recalled was the attack on the Glenanne UDR base on 31 May 1991, in which three UDR soldiers were killed; Paul Blakely, Sidney Hamilton and Robert Crozier. Reatha remembers well visiting all three homes and attending the three funerals all on the same day:

I had just put my car into the garage and had come back into the house and was sitting in this very room; my husband was in bed, when I heard the explosion. The house shook so intensely that my first thoughts were that a device under my car had exploded and I kind of held my breath to see if the wall of the house was going to collapse! I looked out and saw nothing. I went outside and all the neighbours were out to see where the explosion had been. I phoned the base in Armagh to inquire about the location of the bomb, but they had received no word of any explosion. My sister then phoned to ask if it was the base at Glenanne and I phoned the Armagh Base again to check. This time I was told that they thought it was a bomb in transit that had exploded prematurely.

In a few minutes a neighbour phoned to say that the Glenanne base was on fire. I again phoned Armagh and told them it was Glenanne and that I was heading up. Almost immediately the phone rang, it was Armagh to tell me I was not to go to Glenanne but report into Armagh. While I was in the base at Armagh a relative of Agnes Crozier phoned to ask if there was any information on the causalities at the base. At that moment I saw across the desk the Adjutant, who was on a phone call, write down the names of Hamilton, Crozier and Blakely. I asked if anything had happened to those men named on his desk and was told that there was, but that details could not be released because they had not been identified.

I made my way to the Crozier home (they were neighbours of my mother) and I will never forget the scene. Already the house was packed, the Rev Ferguson was there with Agnes and I looked at her and she looked at me and said, "Is it Bobby?" All I could say because of the Army rules was that Bobby was missing and not to build up her hopes. I stayed for a good while and intimated to the Rev Ferguson that there was no hope but that it would be seven o'clock the next morning before there would be any official word. We sent someone to the Blakely home and had great difficult contacting any of the Hamilton family. It was the longest night I ever remember. I waited outside the Crozier home the next morning from 6.50am until I could go in at 7am and tell them that Bobby was dead. However, they already knew, another UDR man's family had heard and phoned to tell them.

Another touching story in connection with the tragedy of the Glenanne murders was when Reatha went out to visit the Blakely family. Paul Blakely who was murdered in the Glenanne bomb had left behind a wife and four very young children, three girls and a boy:

> I would sometimes go out and take one of the Blakely children
> with me to visit another home in Richhill. On one occasion a
> short time after Paul Blakely's murder, when I had one of his
> wee girls with me, I remember well stopping on the way home
> at a filling station to buy her a packet of sweets and I bought
> myself a packet of spearmint sweets. I gave her the sweets and
> set mine in the front of the car and we drove off when she said to
> me, 'Do you like those sweets?' I said I do, and she said, 'Those
> were my daddy's favourite.' She then looked up at the roof of
> the car and said 'I wonder is he getting them in heaven?'

Reatha named many UDR soldiers who had been murdered some on
duty, some at home in front of their families – to name but a few,
Sidney Watt, Joe Reid, (both murdered at their homes in 1973 and
1975 respectively) Tommy Cochrane abducted on his way to work
near Glenanne on 22 October 1982 and his body found five days later,
Stephen McKinney a young man due to start university the Monday
following his murder on the previous Saturday night when he was
ambushed outside his home after coming off his final round of duty
with the UDR.

Apart from these major incidents in which soldiers were killed or
injured, Reatha spoke of the effects of the pressure upon the families
of UDR soldiers:

> Wives and children sometimes did not see their husbands/fathers
> for two or three days at a time. It took its toll upon marriages and
> family life. These men and women gave up a lot to serve their
> country. Part time men served two or three nights a week after a
> days work, sacrificing precious time with their families. They were
> certainly not in it for the money, but all for what?

A LEGACY OF TEARS

As a key personnel within Welfare Staff, Reatha was responsible for visiting the homes of all UDR soldiers who were killed or injured and attending the funerals of murdered soldiers. During her time in this role, there were sixty-eight UDR soldiers from the Armagh Battalion murdered and scores more injured. Visiting these homes and families was no doubt a traumatic and emotional experience, which obviously took it's toll. Reatha simply said, 'you just get the strength.'

> I made it my business to try to do my best for all the families, comfort the bereaved, encourage the injured, fight for pensions and compensation for the victims families. I remember being at the court hearing for compensation with the three widows of the Glenanne bomb and listened to the barrister telling them that £10,000 was all they would get because it was laid down by the NIO. It was hard to take when civilian families and families of republicans had no limit on their compensation. There were families in the 1970's who got only £3,000-£5000 when at the same time there were families of terrorists who got a lot more.

> All of these experiences have been part of the driving force behind my efforts to do something for the victims following my retirement from the UDR.

> When I thought of the people and what they had suffered and their suffering was never ever recognised I wanted to help. People were being killed throughout the years of the Troubles and nobody cared about them or what happened to their families. Mothers left with young children, no husband, no father, no money and struggling to survive. Who cared, the government certainly didn't. Their wider families and colleagues did what they could, perhaps their church helped, but at the end of the day they were really left alone. They were the real victims, the

silent sufferers. Nobody knew their plight, their voices needed to be heard. I decided to do what I could to help, to do something. So I started a Victims Group here in my home.

This Victim's Group began with just four members but it grew rapidly and soon the Group had to move into a hall in Markethill. The Group became known as FAIR. Then in 2000 another Group was formed which became known as, South Armagh Victims Encouraging Recognition. (SAVER) In a very short time the name NAVER was added to include victims from North Armagh.

Bingham House

Saver Naver

The stories in this book have been told by victims who belong to the SAVER/NAVER Victim's Group based in Markethill.

This Group largely owes its existence to the efforts of Reatha Hassan to secure some meaningful help for the victims of terrorism in the area. The group began in Reatha's home in Markethill in 1996. Following discussions with the Victim's Commissioner, Sir Kenneth Bloomfield, and as a consequence of the numbers of victims joining the Group increasing, we moved to a hall in Markethill, and in 1997 we formed the group FAIR.

Following committee discussions and other issues that arose, a new group, SAVER/NAVER was established in 2000 to help bring relief to victims of the 'Troubles' in South and North Armagh and Mid-Ulster, who are suffering from hardship or distress.

A LEGACY OF TEARS

The Group is managed by a committee who meet on a regular basis to offer help and support to each other, to remove fear and restore confidence in members.

The group has grown to over four hundred and eighty members and has been invaluable over the past six years in helping these people to cope with their loss and grief.

Chairperson of the Group, Reatha Hassan commented:

> I'll not say there is great forgiveness with everyone, and lasting peace requires more than words from the IRA. We need genuine reconciliation and trust between communities at ground level and this will take time to establish. While we will never be able to forget that we are victims of the past we are not prisoners to the past and it is our goal to help our victims by means of the diverse activities of the Group. We hope that they will be helped to move forward and be enabled to look to a better future for themselves and for their children - a future free from republican terrorism. This is the very least we and our children deserve.

The SAVER/NAVER Group has embarked upon a major project to construct a memorial wall and garden at their premises at Bingham House, Main Street, Markethill. It is hoped that this project will be completed by 2006.

For further information about the vital work of the Group please visit their website at www.savernaver.com If you wish to contact the Group or make a donation then email them to 'info@savernaver.com' or telephone on 028 3755 2808

SAVER NAVER

We live in Northern Ireland,
With trouble tears and strife,
Where so many hearts are broken,
And so many have lost their life.

For over thirty years now,
We have had this cross to bear,
Not one person out there,
Even seemed to care.

There was no one there to counsel us,
Or help us through these times,
We had to get on with life
With it rolling round our mind.

Then Reatha started SAVER
Now there is NAVER too
So we can help each other,
Our problems to get through.

We have lost a lot of loved ones,
Too many to name them all,
So we would love to build a garden,
Their memories to recall.

We aim to have the garden
Surrounded with stone wall
Where loved ones names can be engraved
And any one can call.

A LEGACY OF TEARS

Without the help of funding,
And those who support our plea
We cannot have our garden
So please give generously.

Pauline Magill

Abbreviations

'B' Specials — ~~Ulster Special Constabulary~~

RUC — Royal Ulster Constabulary

UDR — Ulster Defence Regiment

PSNI — Police Service of Northern Ireland

TA — Territorial Army

SAVER/
NAVER — South Armagh Victims Encouraging
Recognition
North Armagh Victims Encouraging
Recognition

IRA — Irish Republican Army

INLA — Irish National Liberation Army

OTR — On the runs